Capitalism & Christianity

A Moral and Ethical Struggle

by:

Dr. John Laski

© 2008 by John Laski.

All rights reserved. No part of this book may be reproduced, stored in a retrieval system or transmitted in any form or by any means without the prior written permission.

First printing

Final Edit by:

Rezearta Aliaj

Photographs by:

Michele Klastava

ISBN: 9781545318669

Printed in the United States of America

Contents

Introduction

Migration: "Cultures in Motion"

The Bible is an Affront to the Rich

Disdain for the Poor

Hypocrisy

"Pulling on Both Oars"

No Policy Advice in the Bible

Freedom, Trade and Power

Capitalism v. Christianity:
    Historical Re-dux

Capitalism Today

A New Proposition

Calvin Got It Wrong

Theistic v. Vulture Capitalism

Conclusions

Bibliography

About the Author

John Laski grew up in Passaic, New Jersey, during the mid-1950s. Following almost eight years of active duty with the U.S. Navy, much during the Vietnam conflict, John graduated from Salve Regina University with an AS in Criminal Justice, Nyack College with a BS in Organizational Management, later earning an MBA in Finance from St. Thomas Aquinas College. In 2003, John earned a Doctorate in Finance and a second specialization in International Management from Nova Southeastern University. John has worked in international business with Brown & Sharpe Manufacturing, Marubeni Corporation of Japan, UVA Machine Company a subsidiary of the Norden Group of Sweden and later on Wall Street with Merrill Lynch, Citicorp Investment Services, and Northeast Securities. His third career in higher education saw John as an Associate Professor of Finance and founding director of the MBA Program at Nyack College, and Tenured Professor of Finance and International Management at New Jersey City University.

Introduction

Can Capitalism and Christianity Co-Exist?

This book speaks to the moral and ethical dilemma proposed by the seemingly endless conflict of behaviors as they relate to "normal and customary" business practices, the essence or in other words, the so-called purpose of the firm, as described within the context of shareholder wealth maximization theory, and the contrast(s) proposed by the behaviors in the essence of Matthew 5 and Luke 6; specifically, the beatitudes. Do, in fact, the behaviors depicted by Matthew and Luke by design preclude those seeking to be identified as behaving in a Christian-like manner from participation in the Capitalist paradigm? Is the inherent duty of loyalty, as prescribed by these "preferred behaviors," the philosophical trap that precludes being fully compliant to the mission of the firm, thus in effect creating a situation of "duty to multiple masters"? And do the results presented within the context and body of this book, obviate the need to distance Christianity from Capitalism, or at least establish a body of research in support of same? Can there be another version of Capitalism that models the Corporate Wealth Maximization model offered by Moffett; or is that a philosophically watered-down version of the true Capitalist model? In effect and practicality, there can be no absolute loyalty to two "masters," and as such, while further provoking the argument as to whether Capitalism and Christianity can co-exist, it seems inevitable that the conclusions of this book support, and again obviate the need for, further, more in-depth, but clearly more objective research on the part of all parties to the discussion.

I. _Migration: "Cultures in Motion"

Human migration is a fact of history. Peter Stearns suggests that throughout time, peoples have moved for a multiplicity of reasons, involving culture, climate, opportunity, persecution, promise, and much more. The very story of the establishment and evolution of the United States of America is wrapped up in this phenomenon, referred to as "cultures in motion." In fact, my own ancestry bears witness to the idea of flight to promote a better way of life and enjoy greater opportunities. While by no means the first to pursue the dream, my own grandmother, Veronica Kida, left Poland at the age of 13 in 1913, speaking no English, for some of these very reasons. Landing at Ellis Island, she of course was eventually admitted, eventually given citizenship, eventually married, and eventually, the rest became history. Was it the desire to be safe from the impending World War, or was it a chance to make it big in America, or was it something as simple as the need to see ...to see what else is out there; that entrepreneurial and adventurous spirit of

Columbus and De Gama? And further, to borrow and paraphrase the words of Vasile Badaluta, an immigrant who came to America over 30 years ago, drove cabs, swept floors and whatever else before becoming the owner of Stark's Restaurant in NYC, while "one's new country is like a new wife, the ancestral homeland [Romania, in Vasile's case], is like the forever mother."

Imagine the impact of an Iranian diplomat, son of a high-level diplomat, traveling to this land and meeting up with the first- generation daughter of a Polish immigrant at a St. John's University dance, and then marrying to further the next generation of each culture, carrying yet melding the beliefs, cultural distinctives, economics, etc. This was the very story of my mother's sister, my Aunt Mary and her husband, my Uncle Mohsen, second-generation diplomat, ambassador from Iran to the United Nations before the Shah fell. Imagine the culture clash and the broadening of thought that must have occurred.

To add an underscore, my Uncle Mohsen's first cousin, Soraya, was the former wife of the Shah of Iran, at least until it was determined that she could bear no children which, as such, presented the clear problem of succession; all of this obviously before the Islamic—or perhaps Islamicist—Revolution that drove the Shah into exile and gave the world the Ayatollah Khomeini. Talk about "cultures in motion." What are the odds? I wonder if the creative workings of Stephen

King could put together a story such as this one. Jehu Hanciles notes in his work that accompanying these moves are the beliefs, ideas, religious practices and other baggage transported by the movers. Peter Stearns is the one who refers to this phenomenon as "cultures in motion," an entirely appropriate phrase of demographic paradigm shifts: "The movement of peoples has the capacity not only to foster cultural diversity but also to significantly alter demographic, economic, and social structures. This capacity makes it a potent source of social transformation and an active ingredient in the great dramas of history" (Hanciles, 2003, pg. 146). It is completely reasonable to infer, at a minimum, that due to these types of migratory events, whole cultures and cultural behaviors, including those prominently contained within the body of the world's major religions, also move with these migratory patterns. Hanciles suggests that "migration movement was and remains a prime factor in the global spread of world religions ..." (pg. 146)
making special note to Christianity.

However, as I can personally attest, the influences of Islam and Christianity did not fall entirely dichotomously on the ears and hearts of my cousins, Homayoun and Dara. As both Aunt Mary and Uncle Moshen worked to develop a broadness and inclusiveness in their collective lives, and recalling my cousins' acceptance of Islamic ideals and tendencies—

particularly in their early and formative years—it is nothing short of inspiring to find my aunt singing her heart out at Sunday Christian services in Washington, D.C. Inclusiveness ...certainly. And boy, have we come a long way—traveled a long road, whose end, while uncertain, is inclusive of some of the seminal ingredients of upbringing.

The Islamic age is roughly characterized as having occurred from 750 to 1750 A.D. and the significant emergence is again largely attributed to migration, strongly influenced by the Roman and Persian empires. Arguably, it was not until the 16th and 17th centuries that Christianity achieved a somewhat similar presence, and this is largely attributed to the European migrations of the 15th century, as well as the entrance of the wide scope of commerce and maritime activity of the day. Factually, in the 19th century, between 1815 and 1915, pursuant to Hanciles' work in this area, some 50 to 60 million Europeans emigrated overseas. "The export of people was perhaps the single most important dimension of the rise of the West between the sixteenth and twentieth centuries," Hanciles cites of Samuel Huntington's work. As a simple contrivance, if not convenience, to illustrate the point, we can look back to the slave trade, which footed or even founded the GDP of an emerging nation, the United States. Often in my classes I look to the outcomes or effects of something against something else, in effect relating or attempting to relate variables to each other and measure the impacts. Well, simply put, in agrarian America, with its economic roots in the South, GDP might well have been defined as in the words of Adam Smith: "all wealth is the product of labor." And, of course, the argument of Huntington is not missed as an integral part of the emergence and inevitable maturity of the economic growth of the nation. One might even muse over the idea of an entire economic paradigm having been built on the backs of a black counterculture of sorts, never intended to fully emerge and succeed, but on whose backs emerged the greatest economy the world has ever seen. Again, cultures in motion ...what a concept! Perhaps there's another book in this alone.

Thus, we recognize that immigrants travel with their religion— with much more, obviously, but certainly with their religion. "It is central to their way of life and a crucial means of preserving identity as well as homeland connections" (Hanciles, 2003, pg. 147). It is reasonable to connect, then, that this current trend of globalization is and can be linked to the migration tendencies of history, and that the influences that impacted immigration change will likely impact globalization change in a similar manner.

Hanciles suggests that the migratory changes of recent decades have increased to unprecedented levels; that we are, in effect, living in "the age of migration." After all, by the early '90s, he suggests, there were approximately 17 million refugees and asylum seekers in the world, 20 million internally displaced people, 30 million "regular" migrants, and another 30 million migrants with "irregular" status. The combined total is 97 million persons, which represents a doubling of the global migrant population in the space of just five years. Recently, just in the United States there has been an immigration focus on a number approaching 12 to perhaps as much as 20 million, purportedly illegal immigrants from Mexico alone. According to his research, the number of migrants, defined as those who have lived outside their homeland for one year or more, is something approaching 150 million persons.

On a recent trip to Miami to catch a cruise ship to the Western Caribbean, I was poking fun at the announcements at Miami International as they were delivered, with all sincerity, in something I can only describe as a poor attempt to use a kind of hybrid language. Clearly of Latin tongue, the announcer delivered the message that if you were here to catch a cruise ship, you needed a bus voucher to board the bus from the airport, to take you to the cruise ships at the pier downtown. But the message came out something like this: "…if ju need da bus to the boat, ju need have a boucher. No boucher, no bus! No bus, no boat!" And while cheap and obviously offensive to some, my close friend George and I cried, we were laughing so hard. Of course, later that night, on board the Voyager of the Seas, the topic of dinner conversation was that announcement, in the worst attempt to mimic the tone and tenor of that message since Al Pacino did Scarface.

In terms of theories surrounding migration, one referred to as the neoclassical economic perspective explains international migration in terms of the supply and demand of labor. This is very much the current domestic American/Mexican issue. The historical structure approach (allied to the world systems theory) focuses on the unequal distribution of economic and political power. But more recently, the migration systems theory has focused on migration patterns involving specific regions and/or countries, and proposes that "migratory movements generally arise from the existence of prior links between sending and receiving countries based on colonization, political influence, trade, investment and cultural ties"(Hanciles, 2003, pg. 148). One need only look at the influence of Western block nations on the so-called Eastern bloc since the fall of the U.S.S.R. and, arguably, Communism. The re-unification of Germany brought many things, including a virtual paradigm shift in technology and access.

In the early and mid-1980s, under COCOM—which basically ended in 1994—and other international agreements, technology transfer was limited. While working for UVA Machine Company, Bromma, Sweden, we could only ship high-tech fuel injection nozzle bore and seat grinders to Eastern bloc firms in Eastern bloc countries with more dated and limited computer control systems. There was no possibility of shipping five-axis simultaneous control systems to these countries, for what, in essence, was a national security issue. But as immigration ultimately forced influences, and those influences subsequently resulted in major change, the reversal of movements can be defined by the technology movements subsequent to the political and cultural changes of the time. Of course now, basically, every nation has or has access to largely the same technology, with very few restrictions and limitations. Thus the technology edge is slim and very fast moving; again, evidence of cultures, and their resultant behaviors, in motion.

Hanciles suggests that one of the best summary evaluations holds that "the upsurge in migration is due to rapid processes of economic, demographic, social, political, cultural and environmental change, which rise from decolonization, modernization and uneven development"(pg. 148). This analysis also presupposes acceleration into the future, leading to even greater dislocations and changes in societies, leading to even larger patterns of migration. FM2030, renowned futurist, predicts in *Up Wingers* and his other writings that such dislocations and migrations will eventually render borders useless, be they physical, political or cultural. But do these migrations bring peoples closer together, or drive them farther from each other? And, then, exactly how do these migrations or migratory patterns function?

The evidence suggests that due to the wide gap between the highly industrialized "have" nations of the north, and predominantly "have not" under-developed nations of the south, migratory patterns are largely from south to north. Is FM2030's ultimate proposition then reasonable, or even realistic? And if it is any of that, is it largely due to enlightenment, or simply the pursuit of riches; in other words, the search for greed fulfillment? The pressures to migrate seem to emanate from the dichotomy of wealth and resources, wherein the world's richest 1% receive as much income as the poorest 57%. This dichotomous relationship belies the fact that demographic growth and economic development do not correlate well, in positive terms. This is held to be the migration catalyst that will see 95% of all global population growth in developing countries, with Africa as the fastest- growing continent, likely to triple its current population of 800 million people.

In striking contrast lie the developed countries, which comprise 15% of the world's population but account for 60% of its GDP. Developed countries are already exhibiting signs of stagnant or negative population growth, according to the NY Federal Reserve Bank, a theme carried forward in a new soon-to-be-published book on global economic migration *Shantytown* (Laski, expected 2007).

The pre-Perestroika U.S.S.R. experienced an ongoing negative birthrate, such that in terms of economy, it faced the prospect of open borders or mass goods and services importation, but without the base of hard international currency, a mistake the PRC (People's Republic of China) is not replicating. Hanciles cites that in every developed country, the birthrate has dropped below the 2.2 live births per woman of reproductive age, a largely accepted benchmark. Projections of decline continue for Europe, with Germany facing a statistic that suggests half of its adult population will be aged 65 or over by 2030. Germany is the world's third-largest economy, and this presents real economic issues going forward. The U.S. decline has improved to a level just below the replacement rate and continues to improve, but there is little argument that the demographic change caused by the aging and retirement of the "baby boomer" generation is unprecedented and meaningful. Yet in terms of overpopulation, without much argument, the PRC and countries like North Korea seem to lead the way.

The implications of this include that over the next 15 years, Germany will "have to import one million immigrants of working age each year simply to maintain its workforce" (Drucker). Perhaps that immigration will come from both China and North Korea, unless there is no reason to emigrate, which creates an interesting dynamic of its own. After all, the Capitalist greed models are served rather well by the cheap pools of global labor supplied by both PRC and North Korea. An interesting dynamic? To be sure. Prophetic? We'll have to wait and see.

Some issues surrounding these arguably disturbing trends include the idea of sovereign countries like the U.S. erecting "walls" of sorts (to mean physical and political barriers) to stem the impact of this pattern of wholesale migration. In effect, Hanciles refers to this action as one of transforming the world into less of a global village and more of a "gated community." Domestically, the 110th Congress is faced with resolving the "illegal immigration" and open borders issues, spoken of earlier. There is varying support for this "gated community" idea, but the alternatives proposed are so harsh and so costly that it may well be that the U.S. becomes the "gated community" of choice in the coming decade. But the most negative impact or effect by far is cited by many as the great "brain drain." Hanciles states that Africa, for example, has lost about one-third of its skilled people, including 45% of its engineers, to Europe. Indeed, as many as 20% of my current MBA students come directly from or are ancestrally linked to the continent of Africa. The John Stossel ABC piece "Is America Number One" speaks in part to the emigration of entrepreneurs, and the likes of Andy Bechtelstein of Sun Microsystems, and Martine Kempf, who pioneered voice recognition systems, all of whom participated in that great European "brain drain" of the '80s and '90s. This is only a representative sample. And with no immediate desire to return, the migratory patterns described earlier seem to be once again supported by this brain-drain phenomenon.

So among the wide array of influences and impacts lies the fact that a new paradigm, often referred to as "transmigration" (to mean transnational migration), exists, and lends itself to migrants who invest socially, economically and politically in their new societies, and who then typically continue to participate in the daily life of the society from which they emigrated but have not abandoned. Put slightly differently, an African American often maintains their identity as African, not American; a Polish immigrant to America, a Pole rather than an American; Greek, German, Iranian, etc.

A noteworthy example of this concept of "transmigration" can be found in the traditional Western missionary. This is an individual who, in essence, claimed and was claimed by two societies, developing strong ties and commitments to both. This dimension was significantly responsible for the spread of Western culture and ideas, and did impact and shape other societies and cultures to a great extent. Viet Nam is perhaps a glaring, if not the most glaring, example of this particular phenomenon. While many argue the exact dates of involvement in terms of the Viet Nam

War, it is anything but the 1960s and JFK, or even 1950s and Eisenhower. As a matter of fact, there is strong argument and evidence that suggests this most- conquered nation in history, Viet Nam, has been at war since the 1400s, and this started with the culture clash crisis brought about by the European—specifically French—Christian Missionaries, who sought to create change in many areas, culturally, politically and economically, but much surrounding the changes in religion from pagan idolatry to Christianity.

It is further noteworthy that none of the other major religions, according to Hanciles, has matched the Christian missionary mobilization, as evidenced in the Viet Nam struggles of the 15th century, or the continuing spread of Christianity today. Recent inroads have been and continue to be noted by the proselytizing Islamic Imams, as the Islamic culture has grown in major U.S. and European cities, and the number of mosques has increased significantly since the 1970s, but the growth rate is not entirely documented, as many of the Islamic facilities and elements seem to surround, at least anecdotally, an "underground element" of so- called radical Islamists. These are they who are neither desirous of being documented, nor easily documented nor categorized. In any event, we should neither be surprised nor confused as to purpose, since as pointed out in ACTS 17:6 NIV, the faith (Christianity) was barely a decade old when its detractors complained that its adherents were causing trouble "all over the world." Adrian Hasting proffered that even during the difficult periods in Christian history, when survival was not assured, the "universalist momentum" (Hanciles) defied territorial confinement and transcended all human constraints: political, social, and cultural. As such, Christianity is the only world religion to carry the dubious distinction of being a minority faith in its place of origin. Other major religions—Hinduism being one far older, and even the universally equal Islam—have retained their same geographic and cultural centers, but not Christianity.

Clearly, this distinction offers perspective on and insight into the impact of migratory effects on the growth and spread of Christianity and its behaviors. This also provides insights into the potential impacts of the newly identified Islamic migration patterns that have been emerging in the recent decade. Even Kenneth Scott Latourette (1938, pg 3) writes about the thousand years from 500 to 1500 A.D., which saw the entrenchment of Christianity as the faith of Western Europe, as a time of "vast movements of peoples." With this and other inputs, it becomes clear that the future of Christianity is intricately bound up with the emerging non-Western missionary movement. But it is worth noting the extent that it is predominantly non-Western growth that paints the face of global Christianity. It is a face marked by relative poverty and powerlessness, the antithesis to Capitalist wealth and extravagance. The largest share of growth evolves in the areas of those most impoverished and marginalized by society, in the aggregate.

Of course, the thought banging around in my head is that of the reformed prisoner; the one who, when faced with a virtual abyss, finds "Salvation." This is much akin to the imprisoned Paul and the earthquake. The mission's impact, and therefore influence, on culture is by design a driving force to this end, within the context denoted. The growth of Christianity is perhaps the growth of hope against the vast machination of wealth and excess represented by Western Capitalism. As the Great Commission indicates in John 17:18 and 20:21, "As the Father has sent me, I am sending you ..." and pursuant to John Stott, this is indeed the crucial form of the Great Commission, that the mission, and hence the missionaries, must be one of service, and it must be incarnational. Inherent in this is the message that "it is not from the court of Pharaohs that God's laws are revealed, but rather from their slaves" (Hanciles, 2003, pg. 150).

From all of this we can reasonably infer that if, as defined above, migration injects religion or religiosity, and thereby and therein alters social structure, then by design, Capitalism is or may well be at the mercy of Christianity, IF the "cultures in motion" is largely Christian-based. Recent migratory trends, while largely ambiguous and anecdotal to date, suggest that these same recent Islamic migration trends tend to offer insight in this same area; namely, that if this "cultures in motion" perspective can be construed to be Islamic, either in or by design, then the seeds to impact Capitalism have already been sown, as the clear distinctive of Islamist Radicalism seems to include a decadent sort of disdain for Capitalism.

II. _The Bible is an Affront to the Rich

> *"In a time of universal deceit, telling the truth is a revolutionary act"* (George Orwell).

In an article recently published by the End Times Network, wealth is depicted in many forms against the backdrop of Biblical teaching. An argument ensues that suggests "those with little or no money [rise] to a more wholesome, pure and honest level of servitude, implying that those who have been "blessed" with poverty have a less difficult path to God than those with financial substance" (Stevens, pg. 2). A respondent to the article belies that "the real problem lies in the depraved heart of man ...," the notion, of course, being that among other things, it is somehow more spiritual to be poor. Contrast this with the line from the movie *Wall Street*, where Charley Sheen utters "Dad, there is no nobility in poverty ..." (1987). The argument ensues that "it seems that money is the third rail of America's form of Christianity." I suspect that one need only view the behaviors depicted in the movie *Wall Street*, or *The Boiler Room* (2000), to view a glaring, albeit slightly cynical view of what Capitalism has become. In an almost Leona Helmsley-like manner, those with means seem to despise the "have-nots." Michael Douglas, like a king holding court, dismisses the societal systems used as a basis for participation and control of the general public, a.k.a. the masses. Clearly, these behaviors and the subsequent intent cannot be the things of which the great mythology of Christ is made. Thus, even the intuitive and arguably anecdotal observations lead us to conclude disparity, if not outright dichotomy, in terms of behaviors.

Now, in fact, Jesus did not say that it was easier for a camel to go through the eye of a needle than for a poor man to enter into the Kingdom of God, but He did say that about the rich. In Matt. 19:24, we read, "And again I say unto you, it is easier for a camel to go through the eye of a needle, than for a RICH man to enter into the Kingdom of God." And He said it again in Matt. 19:23: "…verily I say unto you, that a RICH man shall hardly enter into the Kingdom of heaven." And if this was not telling enough, Matt. 13:18-22 states, "he also that received seed among the thorns is he that heareth the word; and the care of this world, and the DECEITFULNESS OF RICHES, choke the word, and he becometh unfruitful."

The Bible does not tell the poor "woe unto you that are poor," but "woe unto you that are RICH; for ye have received your consolation." Even Luke gets into the act in recounting, "Woe unto you that are full for ye shall hunger. Woe unto you that laugh now, for ye shall mourn and weep." And again the Bible does not say, "Go now ye poor men, weep and howl for your miseries that shall come upon you. Your poverty has corrupted you …", but it does say that about the RICH. And again, James 5:1-3, Luke 6:20: "…blessed are the POOR …" And then, the Scriptures do not say, "hearken my beloved brethren, hath not God chosen the RICH …"

Let's face it. At the end of the day, the Bible is an affront to the rich! It very clearly favors the poor over the rich. So much for the inclusive nature of Christianity! "For ye see your calling, brethren, how that not many wise men after the flesh, not many mighty, not many noble are called"; "But God hath chosen the foolish things of the world to confound the wise; and God hath chosen the weak things of the world to confound the things which are mighty"; "And base things of the world, and things which are despised, hath God chosen, yea, and things which are not, to bring to naught things that are" (1 Cor. 1:26- 28).

It goes without saying that rich, Capitalist Americans find this very unnerving, if not outright offensive. Even good Sunday churchgoers seeking the "feel good" of Sunday psalms and song, perhaps to wash away a week's worth of "wheeling and dealing," are made uneasy at the prospect of their relative wealth and good fortune. Why? Well, duh, obviously because they are rich! After all, one must be rather callous, I would think, to despair over burning the steaks on the grill, in the face of abject poverty and hunger overwhelming the children of Kenya. And the figure of Christ in all of this would likely not be the one saying, "Give that one to the dog and put on another steak ...oh, and turn down the heat a bit." This includes clerics as well, but certainly applies to the followers, the ones who so loyally attend Robert Schuller's Crystal Cathedral in Garden Grove, California; Joel Osteen's mega-church in Texas; Floyd Flake's Allen AME; the Brooklyn Tabernacle; T.D. Jakes, and the rest who, at least to some end, learn by the example set forth by these seemingly noteworthy "men of the cloth." It is the group that looks to and follows the Pat Robertsons of the world; the Jim and Tammy Faye Bakkers of former PTL fame; the Jim Swaggarts; the Oral Roberts, et al. These all have at least this common denominator: Namely, that they are uneasy in their dichotomous behaviors, which seemingly conflict well with the writings of Matthew and Luke, and therefore "massage" (which is to say stretch and exaggerate) the Biblical perspective, if not only the definition of the rich. How defensive a recent interview I read with Joel Osteen, when he was asked about the huge amounts of wealth being generated by his "franchise." Of course, the public persona and the internal conflict are often disguised by a convenient misinterpretation—or, arguably, a loose interpretation of the scriptures in an effort to mask the conflict and inherent moral/ethical dilemma. They rely on the almost single source of support for extravagance found in Calvin's misguided application of a so-called "Protestant work ethic," an ethic that never truly existed other than by conditions of convenience and with a manipulative end in mind. Indeed, it was one to which so much is applied, to help ease the pain and justify the lack of congruity and transparency that obviates the Biblical dichotomy found in its perspective on the oppression of the poor by the rich. James 2:6: "Do not the RICH men OPPRESS you, and draw you before the judgment seats?" Romans 2:5 is clear on God's wrath in this regard, and the truth of the matter is that only in Western (Capitalist) Christianity would we miss the Biblical point being made. To be a party to this "caste" system, one in which the rich so abuse and take advantage of the poor, seems to me to be difficult to reconcile. Even worse, to be the one in the pulpit on a Sunday morning and to reconcile all of this to me seems to be an effort in futility. It seems as though the new brand of Pharisees has been defined and discovered in the guise of the Western Capitalist Christian establishment, against which Christ speaks, as found in Matt. 23:33, where He uses the analogies of serpents, poisonous snakes and vipers.

Now if, at the end of the day, one cannot find the resemblance to the Gordon Gekko character of the movie *Wall Street* fame, and relate similar characteristics and behaviors found in the extravagant lifestyles of some of the "persons of the cloth" previously mentioned—not to exclude their flocks—then the lack of both objectivity and forthrightness needed to assess at arm's length is unrestrained and, by the way, missing in action, at least from the perspective of this author.

Ultimately, the "end of days" is largely about money, from one perspective or the other. In Rev. 13:16-17, it is very clearly indicated that unless we come to grips with the stranglehold money has on us and our lives, we will never get past what the Bible refers to as the "deception of the end of days." It is noteworthy to suggest that this is largely a problem of Western Capitalist Christianity, as the Shareholder Wealth Maximization theory (SWM) is not universal in either context, or application. The Corporate Wealth Maximization model (CWM) proposed by Michael Moffett, a largely Asian or at least non-American model, is the "kinder, gentler" model often spoken of in terms of *corporate social responsibility*; a model where other stakeholder groups are placed more on par with the shareholders, the clear victors of the SWM paradigm. This opens the door for exploration of what changes might be ultimately considered in terms of reconciliation of these two hugely popular paradigms, Capitalism and Christianity and we will look further to this in later chapters. The same cannot be said of developing nations and that which is spoken of in the arena of "cultures on the move." Perhaps the clearest lesson comes from Luke 9:58: "...foxes have holes, and birds of the air have nests; but the Son of man hath not where to lay his head." In a kind of allegorical way, one might well propose the argument in terms of "best fit"; meaning, where is the fit for those who fail to fit well into the SWM paradigm. And while both texts and authors speak of the emergence of CSR and other evolving social theories that seem to share, if not split, characteristics between competing Capitalist models, the reality at the end of the day is that the Western Capitalist model is what it is ...and the proponents of some "mythical" hybrid of same in fact redefine SWM into something it is not. Thus, it follows logically that advocates of same support not the Western Capitalist model, but a version more centrist and, both economically and politically, positioned somewhere closer to a more socialist or culturally relative model. Again, it is not about good or bad, right or wrong; it's very much about difference or differentiation.

The implications of SWM v. CWM are not lost on this author, either. Recognize, before we too quickly condemn the SWM theory, that it is in fact this economic prescription that has given us the inventions, cures and personifications of greatness that, as a society, we have cheered for the decades this country has been in existence. Even in the movie *Patton* (1970), with George C. Scott, we hear him utter the phrase "America loves a winner and will not tolerate a loser." Well, how many winners would we have to celebrate if the distinctives of success were not the prevalent driving force of the successes touted? Thus, while America cheers a winner, it seems the Bible seems to favor the poor ...often, the loser.

III._Disdain for the Poor

In a system of Capitalist wealth, the almost begrudging welfare provided to seemingly needy individuals pales in comparison to the billions and billions of dollars in "corporate welfare" that the secular, Western Capitalist paradigm receives. The naiveté of the proposition that Capitalism neither breeds nor advocates welfare is pure lunacy. It is a matter of which entity receives it. Even simplistic examples drive the point forcefully. The firm may expense clothing, uniforms, etc., but if I spend money to try to look good at my place of employment, it is with after-tax dollars, with no exemptions. An argument discussed by Hanciles speaks of welfare being quite all right for the rich, but not all right for the poor. Even the so-called *Religious Right*, as it is referred to in Hanciles' paper, tends to support the "free trade" economic policies of what it characterizes as rich corporate sponsors, all the while shipping millions and millions of American jobs out of the United States to the "slave-labor camps" they have set up in the third world. Of course, being a sort of Capitalist, and recognizing firms such as Wal-Mart as little more than conduits between supply and demand—and, of course, on that basis, finding that it is really you and I who are the greedy cause of this phenomenon—it is a hard argument to make, in terms of "slave- labor camps." Hanciles is quick to point to the resemblances between the current "workfare" conditions and those of the 18th century, Calvinist cohorts in England, led by Rev. William Wilberforce, which forced hideous conditions on the starving Irish during the great potato famine. Whether NAFTA or outsourcing to the People's Republic of China (PRC)—or CAFTA or whichever—the objective is clear and synonymous.

It is apparent that these kinds of behaviors tend to support the concept of "gated communities" spoken of earlier in the text, where the collars and cuffs seem not to match in terms of form over substance or, if you prefer, the design vs. the actuality of the situation. Preach a Puritanical moral ethic, while blaming the poor for their own poverty, all the while supporting arguably elitist economic policies that tend to strip the poor of the "living wage" they need to survive and support themselves, at the same time maintaining the Capitalist perspective of shareholder wealth maximization as certainly the rationale, if not simply the justification for same. The utter hypocrisy between the Capitalist paradigm and Christianity, in terms of these behaviors at least, becomes clear; or perhaps, at minimum, less clouded and more transparent. The Capitalist paradigm simply does not support artificial wage floors and ceilings

...and that's just how it is in this Western SWM model. The "invisible hand" of Adam Smith, the free-market arguments of Ronald Reagan: These are the Capitalist tools, and be they effective or not, arguably equitable or not, and almost regardless of outcome, the very intuition of either of these brings forth pangs of resentment and disassociation in the true Western Capitalist.

This is what, according to Hanciles, makes the Christianity of the Western world out to be the sham it has become. A once-compelling argument largely coined during the Reagan presidency is the phrase "trickle-down economics." The basis of support here was found in the higher ingenuity and somewhat elitist knowledge (intellectual property) held by the power brokers of Capitalism: the big business magnates. The basic theory went something like put wealth in their hands (the big business magnates), and with their success will come a "floats all boats" kind of outcome. If these business types are successful, then they must surely hire more and pay more, and thus the outcome will be that "everyone" does well. In a sense, it was kind of a "corporate welfare" argument, or perhaps better called a "corporate workfare" argument, which says as the rich get richer, they need the rest of us peons to do their bidding. As such, we are all brought along by this wave of Capitalistic success. Certainly, one could argue that at least half of the proposition worked ...the 1980s and 1990s saw unprecedented corporate success and growth, and, of course, as grows the corporate success, so grows the individual wealth of the major Capitalists at the helm. The poor did not fare quite as well, especially with the outsourcing for even cheaper sources of labor and even lower wage rates. Unemployment soared, and the aggregate standard of living failed to fully reflect the impact of same, in that the offsets provided by the new wealth, albeit concentrated wealth, sufficiently hooded the vulture. So the economic choices to spur economic growth and activity certainly produced a higher GDP nationally, higher corporate profits and shareholder wealth, but fell short a bit in the arena of the poor. Arguably, trickle-down economics did what it was intended to do ...Hardly a Christ-like endeavor.

It is of note, however, that *poor* is indeed a word—little more than a word to some. To define "poor" is to attempt to reach a sort of consensus that is reached no more easily than most arguments surrounding politics or religion. For example, John Stossel, in his ABC News piece titled "Is America Number One," speaks to the conditions of poverty that exist in the south Bronx—one of the poorest, if not the poorest, congressional districts in the nation—as being a place where while abject poverty and homelessness exists, the word "poor" is applied to those with such accommodations as color televisions, microwave ovens, cable service, one or more cars, and such. He contrasts this application of the word "poor" to the poor of many parts of India, where children live in squalor and eat scraps from garbage dumps and refuse piles to survive. Clearly, the distinctive of poverty, or "poor," is location driven, an underlying force in "cultures in motion"?

There is the often-cited argument about how much various wealthy individuals, the likes of Bill Gates, give to "the poor." But again remember, at the end of the day, without these charitable giving deductions, the government would take at least that much in taxes, and the difference really becomes who, then, gives this money away? Does the donor give it to the government to be "redistributed" to the poor, or some other less than entirely useful purpose, or does the donor give it away in his/her own name and take the credit and reap the more egocentric rewards of "being a nice guy"? Ultimately, do the Bill Gates and Donald Trumps of the world—or, for that matter, the Angelina Jolies and such who have so much to say about world poverty—do they live with, school with, party with, dine with, beach with this element called "the poor"? Or is it an academic argument that ultimately ends with a hot shower and a Malibu beach house view, over filet mignon and Grey Goose dirty martinis? No, I would argue that there is a definite have vs. have-not disdain for the poor. Perhaps the argument proposed by an element of "cultures on the move" is inclusive of the argument that migratory patterns also reflect relative conditions of true poverty vs. rhetorical poverty. Not the rhetorical poverty of the south Bronx, which is more akin to the "keep up with the Joneses" psychology of the '60s, but the true and rampant poverty of Kenya, Viet Nam or some parts of India, to name a few. Not many seem to be moving out of the south Bronx in a big hurry, but rather actively seeking both elicited and, arguably, extorted funds from both government and the Capitalist paradigm, in an effort to bridge the have vs. have-not crevasse and create a better, localized lifestyle at the expense of others. No, there is a definite disdain for the poor, but as to which poor and why is the subject of greater scrutiny, as we may well find it to be the Capitalist retort to the extortive designs of political convenience.

IV:_Hypocrisy

"Woe unto you, scribes and Pharisees, hypocrites, for ye pay tithe of mint and anise and cumin, and have omitted the weightier matters of the law, judgment, mercy, and faith: these ought ye to have done, and not to leave the other undone. Ye blind guides, which strain at a gnat, and swallow a camel" (Matt. 23:23-24). And is this not what the mainstream of Western Christianity is doing here in America? Much to say and of certainty to be said about abortion, about gays and lesbians, about sexual sin, and so-called "family values," but what to say about some of the aforementioned in terms of wealth and such? While in poor taste, and most apologetically to those whom I shall offend in an effort to both convey sentiment and quote accurately, a very well-known, educated, well-spoken and written, accomplished professor, whose name I shall protect for obvious reasons, postulated Christian hypocrisy in the phrase "...love Jesus, hate Niggers." Suffice it to say that Christian hypocrisy today goes well beyond that sentiment, and those abhorrent words. And while I almost choked on my lunch that afternoon at Stark's, his urgent conveyance of at least a portion of his experience in a certain segment of the Christian paradigm reflects the deeply embedded biases that exist to this day, wholly inconsistent with the teachings of Christ (my point here), but very reflective of what should arguably be the dichotomy of business and Christian behaviors. *Christianity Today*, to extend the example, published studies that indicate there is as much drug addiction, divorce, and sexual sin among so-called "born-again" Christians as there is in the general population. Even at Christianity's highest places: Ted Haggard, for example, was recently caught in both homosexual sin accusations, and allegations of drug use and abuse. Of course, he was the commencement speaker at the top Christian liberal arts college in the New York City area, just prior to these most embarrassing releases.

And to all of this, and the much more not spoken of here, the Christ figure's position would be obvious. "Thou hypocrite, first cast out the beam out of thine own eye; and then shalt thou see clearly to cast out the mote out of thy brother's eye" (Mark 7:3-5). Thou hypocrite ...that's what Jesus was saying to the Pharisees. You say one thing and do another! Is this not the very essence of the crevasse between, specifically, the behaviors of both the Capitalists and the Christians? But what I find most intolerant is the Capitalist behaviors adopted by high-profile Christians, the likes of Ted Haggard. Is it not apparent that the incongruity is by design, and that neither shall be able to sufficiently bridge the crevasse until either side shall sufficiently change? Is it an accident that the highest-profile Christians enjoy the highest rewards of Capitalism—namely, wealth? And is it not boldly apparent that changes to behaviors in this land of Capitalist/Christian conundrum are not planned as grounds for change? And is it not this change that alters either paradigm from what it is into something other? Some abstraction? And then, is not the problem indeed obviated by the abdication of one side or the other …of course, the question being which side will abdicate? Let's see …give up Capitalism or give up Christianity? I can see the debate from here.

The recent war between Israel and Lebanon was largely to do with religiosity as much as the Capitalist land "deal" that gave half of Palestine to a permanent homeland for the Israelis, as was the fall of the Shah and the takeover of the Mullahs in Iran. Yes, of course, religious in its overtures, but what of the tremendous wealth and land and the seized bank accounts? So the likelihood of giving up one's faith and religiosity is …what? Was it not only recently that an uproar predicated on cartoons of the Muslim figure Mohammad caused riots and a virtual insurrection in parts of the world? So we bridge this crevasse, this dichotomy of behaviors by the religiosity not being abandoned, and, of course, that leaves the movement at the hands of Capitalists? The money vendors abdicating is most unlikely, and the Christians? The Islamists? The Jews? The Muslims? Well, suffice it to say that

Christianity is growing in many parts of the world, so I do not see an abdication or reversal of fortune (pardon the pun) any time soon. And the reality of Capitalists capitulating significant behavior patterns in the near future is equally unlikely, in my view. After all, there is historical precedent for this.

A telling example to illustrate the inevitability of outcome can be found in the example, if not just, historical account of Charles Fuller. Recognizing, of course, that there now exists the Fuller Theological Seminary in southern California, which is widely supported and endorsed by the National Association of Evangelicals, the history of Charles Fuller and, in a major way, what it took to get to that point in history, is really quite disturbing, or at least arguendo, should be; but it emphasizes and serves to underscore the point that regardless of the best of intentions, there is an inherent inability of these two paradigms, Capitalism and Christianity, to reconcile what is demonstrably un-reconcilable. Fuller's wealth derives from his immense citrus grove holdings in southern California, according to Hanciles. In the 1930s, Fuller was Director and leader of the California Orange Growers Association, whose members' wealth derived from what can only be characterized as certainly cheap, if not almost slave labor. During the Great Depression, families that traveled west to find a better life found the "slave-labor camps" of the California Growers and others, where workers would give up typically half of their paychecks to be able to "squat" on a patch of land, with no toilet facilities, no running water, no electricity of any kind, etc. In other words, half of their paychecks went to Fuller and the other growers for this small patch of ground on which to pitch their tent, nothing else. And those who complained about the perhaps perceived injustice and inequity were blacklisted, labeled as Communists, and run through an arguably corrupt system of local justice which, one could argue, made McCarthy-ism a seemingly righteous standard. In 1936, for example, when the citrus workers went on strike, Fuller and others, backed by Standard Oil of California and others, called in the Orange County Sheriff, according to accounts, and with 400 deputies, they beat, clubbed, tear-gassed, and otherwise abused the defiant workers. Upon being jailed, workers were separated from wives and children, the children literally torn from mothers' arms and placed in "receiving homes" and then later "adopted out," as was the custom in those days. It is hard, if not impossible, to contemplate how an individual the likes of this could possibly have a Christian institution named after him, and the support of the so-called "Christian Right." These are certainly not the behaviors spoken of nor advocated in Matthew 5 and Luke 6. This emphasizes, even illustrates, the inherent dangers found in the Biblical caution and principle of trying to serve two masters. This should convincingly suggest that even the strongest and most well intentioned of us cannot succeed in a conflicting paradigm of dissimilar values, ethics and objectives, particularly when self-interest or conflict of interest enters the fray. To quote S.R. Shearer, pg. 13, "What an unbelievable disgrace and shame to the name of Christ!" Anecdotally, the Fuller seminary is thriving and in full swing as we speak, with multiple campuses in California and other states as well.

The dichotomous personification of this horrible historical event continues to this day, in varying but seemingly continuous form. A glaring example is the importation of "beedis," a type of Indian hand- made—which is to say hand-rolled—cigarette, largely made by the virtually enslaved children who are, in effect, put into bondage until a loan amount paid to insure the family's survival is paid off, or monies advanced against treatment of family illness is paid off, or funds provided as start-up capital for a family business venture is paid off. Children as young as six years old are essentially "traded" by family to suppliers that supply major cigarette firms in India, who command their work, demanding high production rates on a daily basis, for many years until the debt, much akin to a loan shark's "vig," is paid off. And while, in many instances, the owners of such enterprises are not Christian seminary leaders, as was the case with Fuller, Christians, by and large as a group today, seem to find little wrong with this, at least from what we can decipher of the rhetoric from the pulpit on Sunday. Where is the moral outrage? Where is the signature drive to Congressional leaders? Where are the marches, the embargoes, the boycotts? There are countless stories of both child and slave labor in pursuit of profits, similar to the Kathie Lee Gifford sweater stories which, like the Nike story, seem to pop up on a continuing basis. These so-called followers of Christ, if even on Sundays, believe, somewhat tongue in cheek, it is okay to bash people's heads in, literally or figuratively, for the sake of corporate profits, so long as the one doing the bashing is not a homosexual, against abortion, and is for "family values." Nowhere in the Bible can one find even the smallest suggestion that any of the prospects of Capitalism, the tenets of same, or objectives of the system itself are biblically based. So then where are the moral "rightists" when it comes to these atrocities? Even the most absurd interpretations, akin to Jim Jones and Jonestown, Guyana, are devoid of solid Biblical support for any of this type of absurdity. Yet the retorts are mild, a bit dismissive, and arguably very lean in content condemnation.

Central to the system of Capitalism is that the world is and should continue to be divided into the management class, the so-called haves, and the laboring class, the have-nots. This prescription simply does not exist anywhere in the Bible! The fact of the matter is that even the very cold "Calvinist" economic system of Ricardo, Smith and Malthus is based on the primitive and Darwinian system of "survival of the fittest," a truly ruthless fashioning of humanity towards one another.

An argument that surfaces periodically surrounds some provisions of the Old Testament. Let's be clear, even the Old Testament, as in Leviticus, speaks of the Jubilee years (years allotted to the return of property.) Leviticus provides that the land of Israel was to be divided EQUALLY in perpetual allotments to its citizenry. And while envisioning that those families that did not prosper would ultimately have to sell their land, every 15 years the Bible established a "Year of Jubilee," in which everything had to be restored to its original owner. "And ye shall hallow the fifteenth year, and proclaim liberty throughout all the land unto all the inhabitants thereof: it shall be a jubilee [time of rejoicing] unto you; and ye shall return every man unto his possession ..." (Lev.25:10-11, 13, 24). To be most clear on this point, this is the *only* system of economics the Bible ever actually set up. It is the only prescription in Biblical terms for the distribution of wealth. Even the disputed book of Revelations is silent on these matters. The obvious purpose was to prevent accumulation of wealth in the hands of the few, at the expense of the many. There is no provision for this "jubilee behavior" in any part of Western Capitalism. I mean, can you imagine the

SEC—or some other regulatory agency, like the NASDR, the SEC's version of a mafia hitman—calling together all of the Fortune 500 CEOs and stating, "Okay, fellas, next year is year 15 ...we need an equitable distribution plan to return all of your profits and successes of the past decade and a half?" Absolutely laughable!

Thus even the so-called Christian Right, who toil in the name of riches of one sort or another, cannot but be held accountable on this matter and in this regard. As we will see later, the basis on which Calvin's arguably trumped-up, so-called "Protestant work ethic" is a sham. But it is most certainly not Calvinism that marries the Capitalist wealth paradigm to acceptable Christian behaviors.

What becomes apparent is that Christians today seem to have discarded all the Biblical, theological and spiritual arguments against Capitalism, and opted for *pragmatism* (Bowman, 2004). Even Earl Lee, in his work, finds that from the standpoint of ethics, Christianity has been a dismal failure. To me it seems more a disappointment, as what I was seeking, I have ultimately not been able to find, at least vis- à-vis a wealth prescription for acceptable Christian behavior. The ethical implications of money scandals, of sex scandals, of warfare, historical persecution—to name a few—mark historical time and not in terms of isolated incidents, and this continues to this day. The book *Doc* purportedly details how the Mormon Church rallied around and protected a rapist who happened to be an elder of the church. Ted Haggard is now in what is kindly referred to as "restoration," a kind of prescription to restore the cash flows of the pulpit to his able hands in the face of horrendous behaviors. I mean, after all, he chose to be the cleric, the "man of the cloth" vs. I, who chose the path of Capitalism. Both sinners, I hear you say? To be sure! But one is a bit less hypocritical than the other. I'll leave it to your able hands to decide that one.

The argument that this is simply an example of a bad apple or two defies reason in the face of the accumulating data, and speaks nothing of the voluminous accounts of adultery and sex scandals plaguing the Catholic Church and many other Christian denominations in recent years. Lee puts down the argument that Christians by and large are more ethical, in comparing the types of behaviors that drive many to Christianity in the first place. In times of trouble, drinking, marital problems, legal problems, these same are compared to alcoholics and the AA program. Are they cured, or is the behavior temporarily modified? Lee cites Charles Bufe, who in his book quotes studies that indicate there is no greater cure or change in those who attend AA than those who do not. Thus, as we extrapolate the findings, we can also argue that those who attend church and those who do not are likely to enjoy the same or similar behavior modification rates of change, and there is no empirical evidence to suggest otherwise. Lee suggests that so-called non-believers who convert to Christianity often display better behaviors than those purportedly "born again." With this in mind, why do we expect that Christians will be any better able to deal with the impacts and implications of out-of-control Western Capitalism than a non-Christian? It is illogical, at best.

Emma Goldman extols the lack of virtue she finds in Christianity in her work *The Failure of Christianity*. And while describing her perspective of Christ and His teachings as the embodiment of submission, inertia, denial of life (all very harsh claims), she makes claim that arguably great minds like Bauer, Strauss, Renan, Thomas Paine and others refuted what she refers to as the "myth" of Christ a long time ago. Obviously, Christians would and do object to this, and Goldman does seem to have a bit of an agenda. Clearly, the tenets of Christian faith surround, by definition, the idea of a faith commitment. She states that as science takes the place of blind faith, theology loses its hold. And as this may or may not be so, the answer is clearly not to be found in simply aggregating numbers and growth rates, as many lurking variables, such as intelligence, education, wealth and such must be accounted for. She speaks of the Fathers of the Church having the ease to preach the gospel of Christ, as it stands for self-denial, self-abnegation, for penance and regret, and is, in her words, "absolutely inert in the face of every indignity, every outrage imposed upon mankind."

There is a compelling argument here, at least as it embodies and embraces, perhaps wrestles, with Capitalism. Is there not gross indignity to humankind when the outliers include abject poverty on one tail, and living to complete excess on the other? She suggests that Christian religion and morality extol the glory of the hereafter and therefore remain indifferent to the horror of the earth. This begins to sound like the martyrdom-speak of the Islamic fanatics, who are promised 72 virgins and such. A sort of "ends justifies the means" argument cloaked in theocracy? She specifically speaks of the poor as clinging to the promise of the Christian heaven as the home for the old aged, the sanatorium for crippled bodies and weak minds. I cannot say I discard this notion out of hand. She talks of Christ as speaking and preaching sentimental mysticism, obscure and confused ideas that lack originality and vigor. To this, I would only suggest that there has been no other who has made such a mark and maintained such a societal interest through the centuries.

While seemingly harsh and perhaps even devoid of a factual understanding of Christianity, Goldman capitalizes on a key point or two that has been kind of the 900-pound gorilla in the living room that no one is willing to speak about: Namely, that Capitalism and all its behaviors, inclusive of greed, just cannot co-exist with Christianity—at least the purely Western brand of Capitalism, around which industrialized economies are built. To frame it simply, the models are just too dissimilar. The behaviors are too distant. A more "compassionate" Capitalism is not, therefore, Capitalism, especially in the Western paradigm. A more "blind-eyed" Christianity is not, then, Christianity, but a more culturally relative mythology, perhaps with Christian underpinnings. Even in the behaviors demanded of Matthew 5 and Luke 6, "blessed are the meek ...": What a preposterous notion in a Capitalist view! It has been demonstrated again and again that the meek are not likely to inherit anything short of their own disillusionment, and largely the earth has been stolen from the meek by the Capitalist "haves" anyway. Goldman argues that meekness has been the whip that Capitalism and governments have used to force man into dependency, into (his) slave position. And she insists that no other religion has done so much harm or has helped so much in the enslavement of man as the religion of Christ.

To be frank, and at the risk of starting a "holy war" of my own, I am not sure I see this in the face of radical Islam, as evidenced in the disregard for the human condition as recently as 9/11. While there is clearly an argument to be made against the likes of Lee and Goldman and much of what Hanciles has proposed and suggested, the undercurrent to all of this is the disparity in wealth that is largely supported, either directly, in some cases as with Fuller, or more tacitly acquiesced to in terms of the Christian Right's alignment with big business, as in the cases of Joel Osteen, Robert Schuller and Oral Roberts. Reaping big dollars while there is abject poverty, suffering, hunger: This is the 900-pound gorilla in the living room that everyone seems to be ignoring—and conveniently, at that. And this is not the fundamental proposition supported by and argued within the text of the Bible or contemporary, mainstream, Christianity.

V. _"Pulling on Both Oars"

Robert Bachelder takes a much warmer and kinder view of the interrelationship between Capitalism and Christianity. He argues that the churches have determined wrongly that modern political economy is incompatible with Biblical religion and thus to be so easily dismissed from Christian consciousness. He contends that to view the world as if Darwin or Copernicus or Adam Smith never existed is, in his words, "replete with fault" (Bachelder, 1990). He cites the work of the United Church of Christ, which published a paper titled "Christian Faith and Economic Life," declaring that the purpose of the church's political advocacy must be "to achieve the Biblical concept of economic justice." And among others, he cites Leviticus 19:16 and Matthew 19:19, where it is stressed that the importance of community is surpassed only by the obligation to love one's neighbor. And, of course, while subject to vast interpretation, the message can only be clear as to what is contemplated within. Of course, interpretation in the context of such abstraction is everything. Love ...indeed! But what of it? Love means give up your riches? Love means feed the foodless? House the homeless? Clothe the clothes-less? Well, then, it must be that these church leaders do not love very much ...unless it is this egoist type of love manifested in the behaviors of Jimmy Swaggart and Ted Haggard. And then how is it that John Lennon's love is not the love of Christ? Christ right and Lennon wrong? Or is it the other way around? The Koran looks to disposition of the infidel in varying ways, dependent, of course, on interpretation. Do these Muslims really have to kill all of us who are non-Muslim? Or is it sufficient to simply destroy our homes, businesses and ways of life?

A. James Reichley says it well, observing, "Capitalism and theist- humanist religion will always be to some degree in tension ...[but] this tension need not be hostile and may be both socially and morally productive. I find myself in a sort of Andy Rooney conundrum here. I guess somehow the use of the word 'tension' really fails to consume the entirety of the vision I have of abject poverty ...you know, four- year olds living out of garbage heaps in portions of India, and thirteen-year olds hooking on the corners of Sunset Blvd. in Los Angeles. And just blocks away lie the banks that hold the millions of dollars of wealth of successful Capitalists, entrepreneurs and yes, 'men of the cloth.' To me, 'tension' seems to understate the problem. To the extent that it promotes theist-humanist values, religion supplies moral qualities that Capitalism needs for survival and that counter its more dehumanizing tendencies. Capitalism in turn, creates the economic base on which may be built, with guidance from religion and democracy, a more humane society of the kind called for by both Christian and, frankly, Jewish traditions" (Reichley, A.J.). Hmmm …

The idea of incorporating a compromise position of sorts is suggested by Cotton Mather, using the analogy of a person having to pull on both oars in order to reach a destination. And the idea of Gladden's "socialized individual"—which exhorts society at large to balance Capitalism, with its emphasis on self-interest, and religion, with its traditional focus on public welfare—suggests the very type of compromise that has been attempted throughout the 19th century, at least. But the likely outcome is one of continued confusion, coincidental acceptances on minor issues in an effort to stay the resultant nihilism from pulling only on the oar of Capitalism, and "communitarianism," which is really to say Communism, pulling solely on the Christian oar.

Alan Blinder, according to Bob Bachelder, suggests that the test of any proposed economic policy ought to ask: "Does it redistribute wealth from the rich to the poor, and does it improve the market's efficiency?" He cites the Reagan years, when comprehensive tax reform accomplished wealth reduction by closing tax loopholes and then protecting the poor. It raised the personal exemption. D.L. Munby, of the Anglican Bishops' meeting in the 1950s, according to Bachelder, in discussing inflation and such, suggested that "what is needed is not a dose of moral authority, but a careful discrimination to discern the real moral issues involved." James Sanders wrote in Torah and Cannon, according to Bachelder, that "the true prophet does not engage in political diatribe to provide a rallying point for a particular course of action …he questions all the powers that be in the name of the one power beyond them." Again Bachelder cites ethicist John Bennett, who once noted, "The church sometimes needs to emphasize those moral elements which governments are most tempted to neglect." And finally, Stein said, "The relevant question here is whether devoting resources to increasing economic growth is a better way of uplifting the poor than devoting those resources directly to such a purpose."

In one sense, there is an inherent argument of basic finance and economic theory here. If we cite Harvard University as an example, one might argue that due to the wealth accumulation drives of the past decades, and the huge endowment that has resulted, the institution at large could, if it chose, admit all future students on a "full ride," meaning full scholarship, and still not have to invade the principle of the endowment. It does not do this. The Garden State Parkway tolls were set up to pay off the debt associated with its construction, and then were to be removed. They have not been. State-approved gambling in Atlantic City was predicated on the full funding of education principle, whereby and wherein the wealth generation of the casinos would fund improved education in New Jersey. Such promises have been marginally kept, at best. In the context of the conversation of this section of the book, we can allegorically connect the argument proposing the methodology to be employed, in achieving the intended result. It is almost akin to Reagan's "trickle-down economics," which basically argued that if a business is successful, it will hire and support the residuary of employees available for work, in the aggregate, and all will benefit. However, we do know, from the last decade in particular, that as a business thrives in an SWM environment, it recognizes its need to further thrive, and this has resulted in less "trickling down" and more outsourcing being done in the name of low-cost labor. It seems, therefore, that there is likely more pulling on one oar than on both— or perhaps it is pulling on one oar, and one's leg! Without argument, or at least without substantial argument, it seems as though if the two paradigms are to somehow co-exist, this is indeed, at least metaphorically, the right direction …the utility and utilization of borrowing from both arenas. Of course, that leaves the inherent argument that by definition, there needs to be a consensus position or redefinition of Capitalism and Christianity. But redefine which one? Who gets to change? And what are they, then, as entities going forward?

VI._No Policy Advice in the Bible

Religions, throughout their existence, have found it difficult to formulate a balanced approach to wealth and the world of business (Vinten, 2000). In later years, of course, the idea of selling "indulgences" to partially fund the building of Saint Peter's Basilica in Rome may be a glaring exception. And to this day, bingo receipts or profits help fund Catholic education, fees for funerals and Baptisms, First Communions, Confirmations, even Bar Mitzvahs, paying for better seats in Shul—all have demonstrated ways of integrating religion and Capitalism.

I remember as an altar boy at Saint John Kanty Church in Clifton, New Jersey, that the holidays meant "big bucks" for me. In those days, the priests would travel to a predetermined list of houses to bless the house and its holiday food, all of which resulted in a donation to the Church, the priest and, of course, a piece for the altar boy who accompanied the priest. I usually went out with Father Zater or Father Camillus, and basically I made about $5.00 per house. So if we did twenty houses that night, back in the mid-1960s, $100.00 for a night's work was

Capitalism at its finest ...at least as far as I was concerned. It is funny in a way, but I cannot help looking back and thinking that it was this same perspective that the parish and the priest had as well.

Today, one need look only to Robert Schuller's Crystal Cathedral, or Oral Roberts University, and we see an integration of Capitalism and Christianity. Religious texts, both ancient and modern, do not really address the issue of a religious perspective on the world of business and commerce, at least not as the main purpose for which they were written, so interpretation is full of ambiguity and uncertainty, and this certainly applies to issues of money and wealth creation (Vinten, 2000). He argues further that Christians should be fully active in the world of Capitalism, on the basis of two principles: "First, there is a fundamental compatibility between many aspects of a market economy and the Christian faith, which makes it legitimate for Christians to participate. Secondly, because of human sin, we need to be continuously on the alert for the way the system gets skewed to further the interests of the powerful against the powerless" (Harries, 1992, p. 173).

Vinten does point us in the direction of "mission" — this, of course, being an intellectual concept that can be analyzed and discussed somewhat unemotionally. Like strategy, mission is a set of propositions that can be used to guide the policy and behaviors of the firm. It is this latter part, behaviors, which will come into our discussions later, and shall perhaps serve as the final integration medium for two seemingly dichotomous paradigms. After all, "Ask not what your country can do for you, but what you can do for your country" (John F. Kennedy, 1963). Yes, indeed, behaviors—the actions, not the words—are what matter in the final analysis. But Vinten (2000) also criticizes that "miracles have become a billion dollar business in the U.S.A." Steve Martin evidenced this in his somewhat satirical portrayal of a traveling faith healer and preacher (*Leap of Faith*, 1992). And while the context of the comment may be slightly off in terms of direct applicability, it becomes clear that the blurring of the Christian and business or Capitalist lines becomes more myopic as the interaction between both increases. In fact, it is sometimes difficult for ordinary people to believe that there exist the kind of people who are so past all feeling toward their fellow man, and so lacking in any kind of compassion, that they are able to involve themselves in the type of "venal and despicable behavior" that the CIA and shareholders of United Fruit were able to get themselves involved in during the 1950s, for the sake of corporate profits and the "bottom line" (Shearer, 1998). Behaviors, not words …this seems to be key.

For the elite, money-making and the accumulation of wealth has become their raison d'être in life. Right and wrong are determined on very utilitarian or ethical egoistic grounds: namely, that which advances their pecuniary ends is held to be right, while anything that hinders this effort is held to be wrong. Shearer is clear that "wealth makes beasts out of us all." "Money (or the desire for money) has a dangerous way of putting scales on one's eyes, a dangerous way of freezing people's hands, lips and hearts" (1998).

Paul cautioned, "They that will be rich fall into temptation and a snare, and into many foolish and dangerous lusts, which drown men in destruction and perdition" (1 Tim. 6:9). And Peter said of those who desire wealth, "these are wells without water, clouds that are carried (about) with a tempest whom in the midst of darkness is reserved for ever" (2 Pet. 2:17). Many who claim Christ as the most important part of life—David Koch of Koch Industries; David Friess, an investment banker; and countless others—have little remorse for their extreme wealth acquired through ruthless business practices, despite the obvious contradiction to the Bible. It is equally hard to envision Bill Gates, Bill Clinton, Wayne Huizenga, Warren Buffett, or so many others afflicted with the classic moral/ethical dilemma: That being wealth accumulation, and welfare of any in need. The only real concern of such people, Shearer argues, centers on their greedy, self- absorbed lifestyle and preoccupation with piling up ever-greater amounts of material wealth and worldly treasures. C. Wright Mills, now deceased, a professor from Columbia University, wrote,

"The pursuit of the moneyed-life is ...[the elite's] commanding value, in relationship to other morals to which value has declined, so they have become morally ruthless in the pursuit of this moneyed-life." Shearer argues that greed renders those who have been captured by it into empty shells who no longer have substance or meaning to their lives. Madonna, perhaps? Beyonce Knowles? John Kerry? His wife? Ted Kennedy? George Bush?

Mills speaks also of the influence of the social changers of the 1960s, but concludes that while they entertain varying and sometimes different social and religious views, in the end they are committed to Capitalism and free trade, where the money flows, and they detest unionism, Socialism, etc. He argues that eventually the very worst in people will manifest itself, and the resultant shark-like atmosphere in business will become one in which only the treacherous and vicious can survive and prosper. What, then, does this say about the alliance Christians have struck with the corporations of the economic right? Well, if, as the Bible suggests, where money is found, Satan is close by (1 Tim. 6:10), we have our answer.

American Christians have been led to believe that a life of virtue will result in financial success. Of course, aside from the abstraction, the obvious convenience of this type of gospel is very reassuring for a lifetime spent as a ruthless business type, now faced with retirement, and Sunday church services in the face of insecurity about a harsh life and impending death. This is the so-called "Green Gospel" of many born-agains, in particular. But I can show and have seen countless examples of where this "Green Gospel" is pure fantasy. A church that forgives on the basis of giving, calling it repatriation, tithe, restoration or whatever. A so-called Christian organization that puts up standards for acceptance, participation, and ultimate success, but bends these standards conveniently is likely in the pursuit of a pecuniary interest. And individuals who acquire wealth, tithe the minimum, donate little else in terms of time or monetary interest, all towards the end of a luxurious retirement with all the materialistic trappings. Ah yes, the Green Gospel! But we should not lose sight of what Rev. 13:16-17 is all about: "Money is, after all, the basis upon which both small and great, rich and poor, free and bond receive a mark upon their foreheads, and that no man hath the might to buy and sell ..." The bait is the buying and selling; that is what money is all about. "Take heed and beware of covetousness ..." (Luke 12:15); "...they that will be rich fall into temptation and a snare ..." (1 Tim. 6:9). It is noteworthy that money, or the lust for it, is as capable of poisoning born-again evangelicals as the elite and business Capitalists, as well as the "leaders" of both paradigms.

From the beginning, Christianity was a movement of the "little people," the "common folk" and the meek, the unassuming. These were largely people of "no reputation," "no account" and very little money. And Jesus, after all, wasn't born into the moneyed aristocracy; he wasn't a patrician; nor was He even what we would today refer to as middle class, according to Shearer. He was not a businessman, nor an entrepreneur …He was poor …dirt poor. "For ye know the grace of our Lord Jesus Christ, that, though he was rich, yet for our sakes he became poor …" (2 Cor. 8:9). Jesus worked with his hands; he was a laborer. The family into which he was born was of very meager and humble means.

Again, while vilifying the rich, "…woe unto you that are rich, for ye have received your consolation" (Luke 6:24), and in Luke 6:20, "blessed be ye poor, for yours is the kingdom of God," we see no specific direction in Biblical passages to suggest an accepted method of economy. Confusion! Again Luke 6:9 speaks of "the mammon of unrighteousness," which invariably leads away from God. Confusion! 1st Timothy 6:10: "…the love of money is the root of ALL evil …" Even more confusion! We are left to apply all of this to a confusing and arguably treacherous system, in which we are forced to participate. But the anecdotal evidence, again provided by Luke 10:3-4— "carry neither purse, nor scrip (money), nor shoes and salute no man …"—very strongly suggests that the kindness we extend ourselves under the misguided efforts of Calvin and others is, in fact, not at all what was or is contemplated in the Bible. And that is where so many Christians today, per Shearer, want the best of both worlds. But Jesus said, "No man can serve two masters: For either he will hate the one, and love the other, or else he will hold to the one, and despise the other." (Matt. 6:24) It occurs to me in as much as Shearer and other authors of the subject, while having been young and now having grown old, and having seem more Christians and more faith destroyed by a seemingly false yet convenient doctrine when it comes to wealth and money, have come to a point or place where the lines are so blurred so as to provide some type of widely held acceptance of this troublesome dichotomy. And, of course, those we hold up above the simple masses of followers—the T.D. Jakes, and Joel Osteens, and Robert Schullers—offer little by example. Again, CONFUSION!

Doug Bandow (2000) cites Danny Collum, an editor of *Sojourners* who, in the 1980s, complained, "the gross inequalities of wealth and poverty in the U.S. are the natural result of a social, political, and economic system that places the maximization of private profit above all other social goals." This, in fact, parrots the ends of SWM: Maximization of shareholder wealth. The human, social, cultural and other spiritual benefits that would result from a more, arguably, just distribution of wealth and power system will never show up on the quarterly profit and loss statements. But indeed this is by design. Few understand the differences between the two models proposed by Michael Moffett, when comparing a truly Western Capitalist model—the "Shareholder Wealth Maximization" model and the "Corporate Wealth Maximization" model—wherein one advocates solely for the shareholder, and the other for the relative equality of varying stakeholder groups, none to the complete exclusion of the other, as previously mentioned. It is clear in his first Epistle, when the Apostle John wrote, "do not love the world or anything in the world," that he was directing that all not fall into the trap of Capitalism. Likely he was speaking of this SWM or Western brand of Capitalism. Capitalism is indeed an imperfect institution and, arguably, one in which sinful men (meant generically) participate, just like many other institutions, but the differing mandates of the varying systems are clear. And again, the Bible is silent in terms of direction.

Now Bandow suggests that the "spirit of Christian love" cannot be reduced to a political imperative, and I would further argue that nor can it be reduced to a single act, or even series of acts. But neither can it be used to forage the systemic mandates of the varying forms of economy under which society thrives. The Bible does not specifically speak to the proper degree of government intervention in the economy, either. There is no explicit endorsement of *any* type of economic system, neither the varying forms of Capitalism, nor Socialism. In particular, the New Testament is remarkably silent regarding economic policy recommendations. Thus, we are left to interpret which systems are more "consistent" with Biblical teaching. And while this interpretive approach to understanding the Bible and its true meaning is somewhat the norm, in terms of wealth and economies, little need really be interpreted if we look to the overall consistency of the message portrayed in its teachings and culture.

The early Christians, says Bandow, at least in Jerusalem, freely shared what they had with the needy in the community of faith. This, of course, was a very socialist, if not communistic, methodology of economic distribution. However, these acts were voluntary, in that Christ never attempted to forcibly redistribute the assets of either non-Christians or the followers. This is a key distinction. The Apostles also taught that giving, unlike under the Old Testament, was *not* a mandatory act, nor was it mandated that anyone sell their belongings and turn over the proceeds to the body at large. Paul specifically refused to order the members of the church at Corinth to provide aid to the believers in Jerusalem. Paul said, "Each man should give what he has decided in his heart to give but not reluctantly or under compulsion, for God loves a cheerful giver" (2 Corinthians 9:7). That spoken of in 1 Samuel 8:11-18 is another matter, however, and significantly more forceful: "He will take your sons ...daughters, fields, vineyards, olive yards, a tenth of your seed, a tenth of your sheep ..." This is pretty strong stuff, and it sounds very unforgiving and unrelenting.

One resolution, perhaps, is to start with the notion that "God is the owner of all things" (Hardaway, 2003). "For every beast of the forest is Mine, the cattle on a thousand hills. I know of the mountains and everything that moves in the field is Mine. If I were hungry …" (Ps. 50:10). Deut. 14:28-29 warns that "every third year you shall bring out all the tithe of your production …and all shall come and eat and be satisfied." And James 2:14-16 suggests, "what good is it …if a man claims to have faith, but no deeds …" Thus, perhaps an insight into the intent of the New Testament that can be inferred from excerpting many "guidance's" is that all people are to be more or less economically equal. Of course, while this begs definition in the face of the examples set by the so-called "men of the cloth," who "toil" in the name of Jesus, it is clear that this perspective regarding individual financial achievement and success is again called into question. And this alone is sufficient to stand in the face of the Western Capitalist model. Again, as if same were not enough, Leviticus 25 stands in the face of Capitalist models with its Jubilee Years, and 1 Tim. 5:8 warns that one is worse than an infidel if family and relatives are not provided for. So much for nursing homes, or parents living out on the streets in cardboard boxes or the tunnels of the New York City subway system. And while the Bible does not suggest that economic inequality is in itself a violation of Biblical principles, since sometimes poverty can be caused by sloth and irresponsibility, the Bible is very clear about seeking wealth as an end in itself, and speaks harshly to oppression and cruelty as a means for amassing it. If nothing else, this perspective places Capitalism and Christianity in opposing corners of the ring.

Thus, the closest we can come to applying Biblical principles to Capitalism may be found in Hardaway's five principles of the Bible:

1. Provide for the basic material needs of those who cannot provide for themselves.
2. Allow private ownership of property and the means of production, and afford protection to the legitimate owners.
3. Be conducive to creating jobs, which allows people to work and fulfill Biblical obligations to earn their own living.
4. Allow each person to obtain the necessary tools to earn a living.
5. Permit economic inequality, after the needs of the unfortunate have been met, as long as the wealth was not gained through force, etc.

To the extent that this does not mirror the Biblical intent, nor the Capitalist intent, particularly as it is loaded with abstraction and lack of specificity, as well as clarity, there will be continued tension between the two paradigms. But indeed it attempts to embody and capture the spirit perhaps contemplated within the interpretive nature of Scripture, either conveniently, or coincidentally.

VII._Freedom, Trade and Power

Otto Scott (2004) suggests, "In reviewing Christian civilization, it becomes clear that only Christianity fosters individual freedom and limited government"; "Yet in the lands where humanistic socialism (under many names) has triumphed, there is not only no equality, but greater inequities than ever before." It was Christianity that saved the advances and knowledge of the ancient world from complete oblivion. It is this seminal understanding and the attendant interactions that allowed Christian intellectuals and Christian merchants to form, in essence, teams, and together they created that which might be characterized as "modern capitalism" (Max Weber). Of course this view held by Weber may not encompass the entirety of enlightened thought on the subject. One might build a compelling argument about Islam which, being an older brother to Christianity, has perhaps been held out in some sectors to do every bit of what is proposed here. However, it does seem an inescapable coincidence that the world's major industrialized nations have Christianity as their baseline worldview, at least historically. Look at the U.K., the U.S.A.,

Germany, and even Spain and France. Of course, in recent times, as the phenomenon referred to as "cultures in motion" continues via globalization, these trends seem to be in flux, and future outcomes are uncertain.

This new brand of "economic activity," through the early stages of the so-called industrial revolution, which started around 1700 and 1701 with Jethro Tull—of the hydraulic seed planter origin, not the musical group of the '60s—and not the early to mid-1800s, as cited in most history books, gave way to what the Sadler Committee ultimately reported on in 1832. This new paradigm produced cruelty, misery, disease and deformity among the factory children put to work under this new Capitalism. These are hardly Christian tenets. But of noteworthy concern is that Hayek, a Nobel laureate in economics, suggests that much of the socialist interpretation of history, and things asserted as having been of factual basis, have proven to be not facts at all, yet are still being applied and used outside the ranks of professional economic historians, and accepted almost universally as true. In other words, as my students often attempt, there is a widespread "self-need" to react, if only respond, to anecdotal information—unsubstantiated and unsupported, but certainly easy to access and very convenient to utilize. To borrow a quote that I cannot accurately attribute, "we are entitled to our own opinions, but not our own facts," and we often utilize what can best be described as "availability bias." Again, while not my own original thought here, I read fairly recently about the nature of this "availability bias" as that of being information we can most easily access ...that which is readily available, and we use that as our empirical basis for decision-making. Is such the case for this more seemingly liberal translation of what can be described as socialist revisionist history?

Hacker suggests that Marx was entirely wrong in his idea that all challenges were related to the forces of production, and that everything else—morality, law, etc.—was "superstructure." There- fore control of the tools of production was all that was important, and everything else could be swept aside. One might almost look at that perspective today as having substance, certainly in this Western Capitalist model of which we speak. Socialists followed this reasoning, and thereby sought to reduce the rise of entrepreneurs by regulation, and then credited the regulations for improving society and introducing industrialization; again, twisted, but certainly convenient. Even Milton Friedman, in his interview with John Stossel in "Is America Number One," highlights his view on the single most important ingredient to entrepreneurial, and hence economic, success: Economic freedom, of course. As this form of unconstrained or unrestrained economic distribution is inconsistent with socialist systems, we see the obvious dichotomy.

From the 1830s to 1860, agrarian slave-

Capitalists of the South were the dominant economic group in the nation, upon which the nation's GDP relied. For this reason, free trade, cheap transport, low taxes, etc. were bestowed upon this group through legislative and other means. After all, it was, in effect, the "old white guy network" that sat in both houses of Congress, sat on the bench of the United States Supreme Court, and were the great bastions— or is it barons— of industry. But since the Capitalist system by definition does not allow individual components to control the whole, the very concept of trust among this and other groups was, arguably, a socialist myth. This helped mark the decline, at the time, of Capitalism as a theory among American intellectuals, and it served to increase their admiration for Socialism (Scott, 2004). In later years, Socialists began to link their theories to what they began to call "economic freedom." While seemingly flattering, again, Milton Friedman might likely disagree. In this paradigm, the individual was "released" from the "despotism of physical want," and all his needs would be supplied by the government. This is clearly not a Friedman construct. Inherent in this path of thinking was that those who attained wealth had somehow robbed the poor, an argument that is fomented to this day in certain groups; of course these would be the so-called "have-nots," I suspect. The context of this obscure, if not obtuse, brand of "economic freedom" is convincingly distressing, at least to this author. Imagine the concept of freedom against the paradox created by the inherent dependency found in Socialism. Even Stossel's piece speaks to some of the dependencies created in major socialist environments like Europe, Scandinavia and such. Eight-week mandatory vacations, summer plant shutdowns, an inability to remove workers once hired, mandatory paid health care for all; in theory, one might argue, good things, but in practicality, very harsh disincentives to entrepreneurship and innovation, let alone productivity. It is really hard to reconcile the phrases "economic freedom" and "socialistic behavior." They are quite mutually exclusive, unless one enjoins the ideas of hybrid thinking and wild abstraction.

Freedom originally meant release from the orders and coercions of others. In socialist hands, freedom meant this brand of "economic freedom," which was again translated to mean a release from physical want. Clearly one embraces the idea of a release from physical want in a socialist context as an almost absurdity. The very premise of same is the dependence on wealth re-distribution; clearly a socialist view. The goal of this end was accomplished by arguments based on the proposition that private wealth was obtained by theft from the poor. Such arguments, according to Otto, provided a nearly irresistible rationale to all who felt unable to achieve success to the degree or extent they desired. Their disappointments in life were somehow the result of an unjust system, deliberately slanted against them. It is the very underpinning of the argument towards wealth re-distribution. This was popularized in the U.S. in the 1880s by the works of Edward Bellamy, who influenced others, including Theodore Roosevelt and Woodrow Wilson. Today it is the basis for every contrivance in equity to the leg-up mentality of affirmative action. It kind of encompasses the arguments that follow the twisted sort of logic that Johnny is not a multi-millionaire major league pitcher today because the coach back in Little League did not let Johnny have his turn at pitching. The fact that Johnny could barely hold the ball, let alone throw it, of course had little to do with Johnny's poor plight in life now.

In 1913, these trends reached a peak, and the progressive income tax was instituted by constitutional amendment, since the Constitution forbade unequal treatment of citizens. Of course, we see the reasonableness of this argument in the fact that the rich pay more, and the tax breaks, like property tax relief, is scheduled against the rich and skewed in favor of the poor. Again the underlying argument is one based on the philosophy that somehow those less successful, or even those "stolen from" by the very successful, must be sheltered and provided for by the government; a social security blanket of sorts. And since the government really does not generate nickel one, the money for this re-distribution effort must come from someplace, and that place is, progressively, from those who have.

The central bank, a.k.a. the Federal Reserve System, was established, and states' rights were arguably weakened by this action. The Federal Trade Commission was established, and the nation got used to the idea of reduced rights when then-President Wilson suspended many individual and states' rights, alleging national security, due to the onset of World War I. Meanwhile, in Russia, Lenin, Trotsky and others proceeded to turn back the clock of history to what some considered pagan times. The government, through fear and other arguably repressive tactics, established an environment of no God recognition, no right of religion, no individual people's rights, and no rights, basically, of any sort. This was hailed by Socialists as a triumph of their ideas, and the U.S.S.R. was considered the first true endeavor at delivering a completely planned economy and political system. This system exists today in India, Cuba, People's Republic of China and others: Planned economies, along with the huge, supportive bureaucracies needed to implement and sustain such an environment. Of course, as in the cases of Venezuela and Cuba, what the government lacks, it simply "acquires." The citizens soon found, however, that no choice meant no choice ...no choice of jobs, doctors, living quarters, travel, occupation; no right to provide charity; no right to hire others or sell property, often to even own property. Private property rights were never a cornerstone of Socialism or Communism. The underlying theme to all of this was the underlying argument of a belief in "equality of condition" for all. If anyone truly believes this is equality, then much more is needed than a simple repartee between reader and author.

Arguably, then, only Christianity was left to develop Capitalism
...and thus, only Christian-based Capitalism provided man with the freedom to work at occupations of his own choosing, in peaceful efforts of his planning, free from coercion and tyranny. The same way that the Renaissance despots arose and took away Christian-based freedoms, and the way the Age of Enlightenment destroyed ancient freedoms, was, and arguably is, being replayed in the arena of modern-day Socialism, which is re-introducing ancient slavery through globalization and its subsequent effects. Yet since the Protestant Reformation, Christianity has been very slow to perceive this peril and remains remarkably silent about the persecution of fellow Christians in largely totalitarian regimes of control, as in the case of the People's Republic of China. Much like the sins of the Roman Catholic Church in the face of the Holocaust, there is much silence, much acquiescence.

According to Dr. Charles Mercieca, Capitalism contradicts Christianity. Capitalism is aligned with consumerism, and not with Socialism. Socialism is aligned with the Biblical perspectives of equal treatment or condition, but what then of the argument of Otto's loss of freedoms, described earlier? Capitalism advocates building up never-ending amounts of capital, while the Bible speaks of avoiding comfort, gluttony, and worldly pleasure. It seems as though these contradicting elements prevent the human soul from assimilating itself with God. The Capitalism advocated, in a sense, by Christian teaching is also faced with the dichotomy of social living and giving, clearly not Capitalist tendencies. There must be something missing here…

CAPITALISM & CHRISTIANITY: A MORAL AND ETHICAL STRUGGLE

CAPITALISM & CHRISTIANITY: A MORAL AND ETHICAL STRUGGLE

CAPITALISM & CHRISTIANITY: A MORAL AND ETHICAL STRUGGLE

CAPITALISM & CHRISTIANITY: A MORAL AND ETHICAL STRUGGLE

VIII. Capitalism v. Christianity: Historical Redux

For most of its 2,000-year history, Christianity not only frowned on Capitalism, but banned it. Capitalism is making money with money; interest, capital gains ...everything we call "unearned income." Even the idea of buying and selling at a profit was looked down on by Christianity, at least historically.

The law against charging interest goes back to Exodus 22:24-25: "If you lend money to one of your poor neighbors among my people, you shall not act like an extortioner toward him by demanding interest from him." This prohibition is repeated twenty-two times in the Old Testament alone. Proverbs 28:8 says, "He who increases his wealth by interest and overcharge amasses it for someone else who will bestow it on the poor." Deuteronomy 15:1-11 orders the cancellation of all debts at the end of every seventh year. James 5:1 says, "Next a word to you who are rich. Weep and wail over the miserable fate overtaking you: your riches ...will be evidence against you and consume your flesh like fire ...You have lived on the land in wanton luxury, gorging yourselves ...and on the day appointed for your slaughter." Matthew 19:21-24: "if you wish to be perfect, go, sell what you have and give to the poor, and you will have treasure in heaven. Again I say to you, it is easier for a camel ...to enter the Kingdom of God."

The early Christians took this very seriously. The first-century Didache said, "Do not claim that anything is your own." Around the year 200, Clement said, "All possessions are by nature unrighteous; when one possesses them for personal advantage and does not bring them into the common stock for those in need." St. Augustine said, "Business itself is evil." Jerome said, "A man who is a merchant can seldom please God."

For 1,500 years, the church banned charging interest. The irony is that the Biblical passages against interest are all in the Hebrew Scriptures. Stereotypes exist to this day that suggest the ethnicity of being of Hebrew descent somehow predisposes one to business acumen and success. In the 16th century, a merchant in Boston was criminally charged for usury for charging 2% higher than allowed by law ...a 6% mark-up vs. 4%. But the fact that he was allowed to make a profit at all was the direct result of the Protestant Reformation. Thus one might argue that Martin Luther was about more than just doctrinal issues, surrounding a strict interpretation and reliance of the Bible, versus the other apostolic positions of the day emanating from Vatican City. Was Martin Luther a Capitalist at heart? Were his true desires more pecuniary than doctrinal? Was he perhaps even the first Gordon Gekko (the movie *Wall Street*) of history?

In 1931, Pope Pius XI spoke out against the concentration of power as the result of a free market, and Pope John Paul II spoke out prior to his death, in more recent years, about the dangers of unbridled Capitalism. It is ironic that the Protestants, who are so literal about the Bible in matters of sexual practice and such, are so unable to explain away their interactions with Biblical prohibitions regarding economic activities. And while there is little argument about the truly interpretive nature of the Bible, just as there is in terms of the Koran, there seems to be nothing but a coincidental convenience of outcome in terms of this dichotomy.

In medieval society, serving the social order was an act of obedience to God. Economic activities that disturbed this order, especially usury and avarice, were widely condemned. It was felt that these activities could divert one's consciousness away from God and toward oneself. Even Luther's emphasis on vocation and the importance of earthly life was not intended to legitimize Capitalism, but rather to motivate people to fulfill, to the best of their abilities, their social obligations. No, I suspect Luther was not really a Capitalist at heart as much as a rebel, dealing with maverick ideas and tendencies on more levels than simply scriptural. An egoist? To be certain. A radical? Without question. A Capitalist? The jury is still out on this one.

Richard Tawney suggests that Calvin did for the Christian bourgeoisie what Marx did for the Proletariat. Calvin viewed personal wealth, interest, private property and such as a sign of God's election and of being chosen by God as one of his stewards of creation (Weber, 1958). Calvin did caution against the danger inherent in Capitalism; namely, diverting consciousness away from the glorification of God. But then hereto, how do we begin to add dimension and definition to this abstraction? What exactly is this glorification of which we speak? Perhaps more importantly, what is it not? And while not being told directly to shy away from making a profit, believers were told to use their wealth in ways not distracting from the Kingdom of God. Again, what does this really mean, in a nuts-and-bolts kind of way? Thus, the early generations at least of "Reformists" saw Capitalism as compatible with religion. Why not? There was little in place to dissuade such an argument. The Calvinists were not looking at Capitalism in the light of it being or becoming the glorification and sanctification of unbridled self-interest and egocentrism at that point. But then, it sort of worked out well that way, didn't it?

The separation of church and state became a larger issue as the result of the multiple and continuing denominational splits that evidenced the struggles after the Reformation. Just the sheer number of splits made it impractical, if not impossible, for the state to claim a theological legitimization of its actions without getting pulled into the same rivalries as those going on between the various religious factions. Thus the state was forced into the position of taking on "modern rationality" as its moral umbrella. A compelling argument can and is made that as much as anything, Luther and the Reformation are responsible for this split between state and religion or religious practice. Objective evidence and logical thinking became the cornerstones of modern rationality. To a very great degree, this is the ethical system that survives today. This forced, among many other things, economists to stop talking in terms of "ultimate ends and moral dimensions" of economic activity, and thus began the focus on the mechanics of what is now modern economy. Self- command was, for example, reduced to self-interest, and this ultimately equated with rational behavior (Dordrecht, 1994).

Currently, the newly revitalized debate regarding the moral direction of business and social responsibility testifies to the likely end of the results of the Reformist debacle that ended with "modern rationality." One might rather strongly and convincingly argue that the "Reformists" are to blame for the avarice and greed of modern times. The doctrinal debate over Christian ethics in terms of vocation, stewardship, and justice usually result in the inability to differentiate Christian ethics from philosophical ethics. When basing moral guidelines or principles on de-contextualized parts of Scripture, clearly the advantage of excerpting, the results seem lifeless and legalistic, and not easily defended when challenged. The basic argument that God demands it is lost in the maze of abstraction and rhetoric. And the rancor of the existence-of-God debate has become un-historically vicious. The author has long maintained that the more difficult and specific the argument, the quicker the flight to abstraction. Stanley Hauerwas argues that "the more we try to mine scripture for a workable ethic, the more we are drawn to separate such an ethic from the understanding of salvation that makes such an ethic intelligible in the first place" (1981). Adhering to a Christian ethic is not the same as adhering to a set of Christian moral values. Jesus denounced the very idea of equating understanding to a set of rules and regulations. What is expressed through the stories of Jesus and the people of God is a comprehensive understanding of reality (Rossouw, 1994). Most theological training grossly neglects a theoretical perspective on economics and business, perhaps largely due to the lack of positive Biblical guidance in terms of same. The author and Dr. David Schroeder, former President of the Alliance Theological Seminary, have discussed this very issue on many occasions. This understanding, the implications of business ethics and such, is crucial if clergy are to intervene in a meaningful way in this paradox. The responsibility of the church is, as much as anything, to prevent social rejection and neglect of those who are not able to compete in the marketplace. This is completely counter-intuitive to the Western Capitalist mentality, a mentality that some attribute directly to the Reformation.

At the end of the day, a strong argument can be made that Christianity is either an amalgam of pagan religions, picking the most successful features from each, or the result of incorporating the utilities of some of the world's great mythologies (Campbell, 1997): the Adonis story of more than 2000 BC; Horus of 1550 BC; Krishna, 1200 BC; Indra, 725 BC; Buddha; Mithra, 600 BC; Quirinius, 506 BC; Attis, 200 BC. There are twenty crucified savior/God/resurrection myths from the Middle East that predate Jesus, and all incorporate several similarities found in the story of Jesus. The early Christians incorporated the most interesting components of the stories of the aforementioned into a story not remarkably different from any one of the above. Authors like Abelard Reuchlin write about the so-called "Christ myth" as having been assembled by Arrius Calpurnius Piso to disrupt and confuse the Jewish rabbis of the day, who were resisting Roman authority. And the suggestion ensues that these stories were certainly known to the writers of the

Gospels ...

Thus, it becomes important from many venues that the authenticity of intent, not just in matters of sexuality and lifestyle, but of economics, wealth, etc. be applied not through the eye of convenience based on a misinterpretation of Calvinist ideas, and even ideas surrounding the Protestant Reformation, but on the entirety of the historical chain of humanist welfare prescriptions, including, but not limited to, taking care of the poor, and not attempting to gain financial advantage over those who either cannot compete or suffer downturns in life. This is clearly not the Western Capitalist intent or model. This is evidently in contradiction with the prescriptions offered throughout the New Testament. Therefore, this clearly presents a dichotomous conflict between the venues of Capitalism and Christianity, both historically and going forward. The debate rages on!

IX._Capitalism Today

In short, and simply put, I have had it with institutional religion, but I am not prepared to give up on my faith commitment to Jesus Christ. I will not blame Christ the historical figure, the mythological figure, or even Christ the figure of faith with whom I was raised, for the inherent garbage that sundry, albeit well-intentioned, and even evil people alike have built up around His memory and His teachings ("Christianity in America," 2003). This "Liberation Theology" that is so conveniently placed in the context of "modern Evangelical Christendom" is baloney. A couple of facts to contend with: Jesus Christ is not a sexist, thus why a glass ceiling at all? Jesus Christ is neither a nationalist nor a warmonger, thus why the ongoing battles of ideology in the Middle East and elsewhere? *Jesus Christ is not a Capitalist.* He somewhat famously berated lawyers in the Book of John, and did command that (we) "render unto Caesar that which belongs to Caesar, and to give unto God that what belongs to God." Further, Jesus Christ was not a stockbroker nor a lawyer nor a banker, but a carpenter ...in other words, a common laborer. Jesus Christ preaches not dividends and wealth, pecuniary rewards and property, but humanity, generosity, and abundant living.

Western Capitalism is, without much argument, the greatest machination of the Pharisees to date, and very much the antithesis of Christian behaviors. Despite what we think when we send money overseas or put alms in the poor box, and send our sons and daughters out as missionaries to faraway lands, they are not changing anything until they change the root causes of the problems. This cannot happen as long as Capitalism exists in this paradigm in its present form. Capitalism—for all else it may or may not be—is, at the end of the day, very frankly, the ultimate most anti-democratic, anti-human, and anti-God econometric system ever devised. It is harsh, it is cold, it is cruel, it is unequal, it is unrelenting, it is discriminating, it is entrepreneurial, it is productive, it is resourceful, and many other condemnations as well as accolades. Is it really likely that this is what Reformist Luther had in mind? Is this the paradigm that Calvin intended to build? Clearly the Vatican has taken a sharp stance against unbridled Capitalism through the words of the late Pontiff, John Paul II. Yet we cannot connect that our decaying morality is directly linked to Capitalist behaviors? Absolutely mind-boggling!

I have two sons, both of whom I love dearly. Yet the lack of lavish upbringing in their lives does not reflect an adequate rendering or understanding of what it is to earn a dollar, what it is to do without, and what it is to be truly poor. Between Dave Chappelle, BET, MTV and others, I truly believe they accept that if you rap a bit, just kind of show up, and make friends, you are entitled to and will ultimately receive mansions, fast cars, jewelry, sexy women and such. Bling bling!

Yet this is what Western Capitalism holds for us, at least in terms of television and media influence, it seems. It is little wonder that other societies see the decadence of the West as a threat to more culturally stable lifestyles; little wonder that other societies see the flaws and faults of Capitalism as actionable in the context of health care, financial lobbying, globalization and such. Of course, nothing justifies the fanaticism of radical elements of both culture and religion, but this Capitalist paradigm, for all of its successes, certainly leaves one wondering about some of its abysmal failures as well.

And while authors speak of Capitalism in one generic, we must recognize differing types or models of Capitalism; there is the Western Shareholder Wealth Maximization (SWM) model, where shareholders are king, and the Corporate Wealth Maximization (CWM) model, which treats multiple stakeholder groups with greater equity than the Western model, which is solely shareholder wealth driven. Perhaps not the context in which Michael Moffett intended, at the end of the day, SWM Capitalism today and the Christian mandates of the Bible are incongruent and wholly inconsistent, in terms of intent, with each other. The culture of synergy of church and corporate business, a.k.a. "Christianity Incorporated," is a corruption far more malignant than sexual abuse (McCarraher, 2002).

But Capitalism today, in its varying forms, clearly is not all bad. It is this paradigm that has delivered anything and everything from penicillin to the CAT scan; DVD to a cure for STD; space shuttles to iPods, and just about everything we see that produces good and comfort, and eases distress. Is it not the uniquely Capitalist paradigm that produces the technology for information access via the Internet, and communication with the kids halfway around the planet? Is it not the innovativeness of this paradigm that has delivered Michael Jordan, and the technology to bridge the River Jordan? Clearly much good comes from Milton Friedman's version of "economic freedom" and, like with so many things, it is the abuse that incurs the negative stereotypes and generalizations we try to avoid.

Yes, Capitalism today is the life-saving technology in the Cardiac Cath Lab at Cornell, which has allowed this author to write this book. For any negative thing I have ever written about Capitalists or Capitalism, on 9/11, a year to the day after the horror of the World Trade Center collapses, yours truly underwent an emergency cath procedure at Cornell by Dr. Bergman, one of my most favorite people on this planet. Despite his

"House-like" qualities as a physician, his skills in locating and dealing with an eclusion in the LAD (lower anterior descending) artery, the so-called "widow-maker's" syndrome—well, suffice it to say, I was never so grateful for the incentives and success of Capitalism, without which such a condition would likely have been a death sentence. So trust me when I suggest to you that modern Capitalism is not by any stretch a necessarily bad thing. An egoist perspective, I am sure ...and your reasons would be?

X._A New Proposition

Compassionate Capitalism, by Rob Moll, is arguably an abstraction of the underlying Western Capitalism model. But slowly, says Moll, the idea of fair trade is catching on among Christians, as not only a way to support mission activities but also for providing jobs to the poor. Further, the proposition suggests building long-term relationships with workers, sort of a Randy Pohlman, value over time proposition, and notes the degree to which a fair wage can impact and change a person's life. Of course, the immediate concern in this Capitalist model stems from the implementation and use of wage floors and ceilings. Jesse Jackson used to argue that there is no ceiling for the rich and no floor for the poor. These contrivances fly against the main cord of Capitalist economic distribution theory. The invisible hand, supply and demand, a self-correcting and highly efficient market: This is Capitalism, not the socially secure prospects of wage floors and artificial price ceilings and such. This is often the critical issue of social policy between so-called Capitalist Conservatives and Social Liberals; of course, this again presents the out-of-focus perspective of exactly where the so-called Conservative Christians fit in all of this, since the policy is liberal and the largely Evangelical Christian view is generally conservative. More uncertainty, more abstraction ...Can a Christian really be a conservative, or is that a contradiction in terms?

Moll points out that fair trade costs more. You could go out there and get the same item for a third less, but now we know what happens to the people who produce that item, the well-publicized cases of child labor, peasant wage rates and long hours in unsafe environments; they are basically hand-to-mouth, if they are lucky. It is the Kathie Lee Gifford story—the sweater and the labor conditions that produced it so cheaply. I use in my classes the example of the

$11.00 shovel. Wal-Mart, the company it seems so many love to hate, is in actuality only the conduit between the forces of supply and demand. The efficiencies Wal-Mart builds into its supply chain are reflected in its value chain and its value proposition to its owners, the shareholders. But again, at the end of the day, if you and I chose to buy the $40.00 shovel made here in the U.S.A. by union labor, instead of the $11.00 shovel made in some remote global village by underage children with one eye and one leg, working 26 hours per day ...you get the idea! If you and I were buying the $40.00 shovel and not the

$11.00 shovel, there would be little debate about this, and we would not be discussing it now.

Karl Marx's goal was ultimately to have Capitalism destroy itself in terms of private ownership through increased centralization of wealth, until ultimately it became a social state. There would likely be a "French Revolution" of sorts, and the Proletariat would re-enact history and the Bourgeoisie would stand up, revolt, storm the Bastille

...There is even the compelling argument by current economists surrounding a more "let them eat cake" approach, where eventually the super-rich, by then in a class by themselves—small as it may be in number—would ultimately be overthrown by the modern-day "proletariat," in a French Revolutionary kind of drama. In a discussion about the economics of the Balkans with Dr. Nicholas Pappavlassopoulos, my mentor in terms of finance, a VP at Moody's New York, and Professor of Finance at Saint Thomas Aquinas College, this is an event to plan for in the not-too-distant future.

Books written about Capitalism from the socialist point of view tend to define Capitalism as a greedy, self-serving way of accumulating wealth at the expense of others. From a more moderate humanist point of view, Capitalism is held to be a system of more good features than bad—a sort of utilitarian view, in that it has tremendous power to help the poor by an outpouring of accumulated wealth in the hands of a few. Of course, the real cause and effect relationships surrounding such a blind-benevolence type of social self-help are not really often explored, and nor are the pitfalls to such ad hoc distribution systems. The fact that the funds contemplated for social distribution by the wealthy would otherwise be taken in taxes and thus give the government the capacity to redistribute belies the true agenda of the wealthy; namely, acquire further stature by seeming to be socially conscious, and distribute what would be otherwise lost to government and social need, anyway. Socialism, on the other hand, is a way of mass or group or government control of wealth; thus, a less likely outcome vis-à-vis this outpouring of wealth. In either eventuality, the system is one thing, the actual distribution is another. Again, despite the pitfalls, Capitalist societies enjoy more state-of-the-art medical care, and often have more CAT scans in one state than an entire nation. Specialists and appointments are quicker to get and patients' needs are better treated than in the seemingly more socially friendly systems. With these and so many more examples, it hardly seems as though this redistribution-of-wealth type of society is the way to go. James Doti (1982) speaks to Adam Smith's Wealth of Nations as an economic system based on self-interest. He notes Smith's words that it is not from the benevolence of the butcher, the brewer, or the baker that we expect our dinner, but from their regard for their own interest. We address ourselves not to their humanity but to their self- love, and never talk to them of our own necessities, but of their advantages (Smith, 1937). Thus the forces of self-interest determine individual actions. The author, again, has long held that we are all motivated by our own self-interest. It is difficult to reconcile this practical religion of Capitalist societies, however, with any system of thought or morality that can be described as Christian. Christ taught that love and charity towards others, not self-interest and self-love, should guide an individual's actions. The contemporaneous dichotomy of this alone is glaringly obvious.

Christ also taught us to "be on your guard against avarice of any kind, for a man's life is not made secure by what he owns, even when he has more than he needs" (Luke XII: 15-18). Christ's message seems to conflict, quite obviously, with Adam Smith's belief that personal gain should be given free rein in society: "Every individual necessarily labors to render the annual revenue of the society, as great as he can. He generally, indeed, neither intends to promote the public interest, nor knows how much he is promoting it …he intends only his own gain, and he is in this, as in many other cases, led by an invisible hand to promote an end which was no part of his intention" (Smith, 1937). The less-than-transparent arguments surrounding the "economic effect" of this greedy behavior are, in many eyes, simply political fodder. Is it really that I intended to help society in some conscious way when I purchased my third Mercedes Benz? Was it my primary or even conscious motivation, for that matter, that the taxes paid would do social good? Of course not! It was all about me, my needs and desires, with perhaps even a momentary glance of disdain at the fact that I had to pay tax at all.

But while Capitalists, especially Western Capitalists motivated by greed, seek their own gain by maximizing profits, there is an argument to be made to suggest this Reagan-motivated "trickle- down economics" theory has merit. And if, indeed, there is any truth to that model, then tangible outcomes and results are enjoyed as a result of this greedy, Capitalist behavior. Thus, living a life based on greed, which appears to be the antithesis of Christian morality, one can do quite well in accomplishing the goal set forth above—that is, to better society and benefit one's fellow human beings. After all, were it not for this "greed," we would not have clock radios, disposable diapers, or even water in Southern California (Doti, 1982). These are indeed the outcomes, or by-products, of greedy, Capitalist behavior. Again, like my personal experience with Cornell, I am down with this greedy Capitalism stuff! Self-interest, I think?

A quite divergent, if not unique, perspective is offered by Cronk. He suggests that although we still claim allegiance to the Christian ethic, religion is no longer the active cultural mythology controlling our lives. Science has replaced religion as the active belief system of Western society. Much of what goes on in the name of Christianity today is retrogressive avoidance of the nihilism confronting post- modern America. Blind loyalty to irrelevant Christian dogma is a measure of the desperation and sense of helplessness that individuals feel in a world controlled by money, technology and corporate politics. I cannot say that I entirely disagree. I hear quite frequently at the university how one of my students is just going to have to pray harder or pray more in the face of some mountainous obstacle facing them. It brings to mind the admonition of the Gene Hackman preacher role in the movie *Poseidon Adventure*, where he is lecturing the other pastor that one could wear one's knees out praying to God, and must therefore take a more proactive and participatory role in things. The underlying theme of personal responsibility seems to reject the reliance purely on the reigning mythology in favor of a more proactive stance.

Cronk indicates that in the 16th century, society began to turn from the transformative experiences of Catholicism to the ideological rationalizations of Calvinism for confirmation of ethical values. In recent decades, society has fallen prey to institutionalized bigotry, self-serving religions and economic Darwinism. How, for example, does the individual find truth or meaning in life, or make intelligent and informed decisions, with a heavily censored and propagandized education? The pulpit also has been used to sway the public to take positions diametrically opposed to the intent of Christian doctrine. The morality of entrepreneurial Capitalism has given way to the interests of corporate Capitalism. Despite constitutional guarantees to the contrary, we are subjected to political and economic systems bent on exploiting the rights of the many to profit the few. Cronk supports that the American ethic is the business ethic. He indicates that you can feed the public poison if it turns a buck. American society, while paying lip service to a religious ethic, pursues policies offering economic stability, not salvation. An example is the softening resistance with missionaries and Coca-Cola: Western interests exploit cheap labor sources in the name of God and the American way.

The flaw in the psychology of Christianity, according to Nietzsche, is rancor. If there is no enemy, we will make one up: Someone must be made responsible for the suffering endured. Can the Christian paradigm develop a political and economic system where the rich do not suppress the poor? Importantly, do they even want to? It appears, at least in one argument, that the key for establishing a successful society is for personal values to be the same as society's values. This is a tough proposition in a paradigm where it often seems as though the metric of success, on almost every level, is monetary and individualistic. In a recent "discussion" (which is to say argument) with my older son, I criticized the outrageous behavior of a particularly wealthy and well-known basketball star, Dennis Rodman. And the acceptance and recognition of the rightness and correctness of his behavior, as justified by my son, was the fact that he (the player) was rich beyond compare, and thus correct. Unfortunately, it seems as though society has substituted wealth, consumer gratification and the business ethic for the ideals necessary to produce humanitarian ethical codes.

Cronk argues that the exploitive politics of monopolistic Capitalism will continue to suppress the rights of non-Western countries and allow big business to ravage the environment under the guise of free-trade and Christian morality. These policies, while clearly supportive of the Western Capitalist model, allow for a type of moral escapism from the responsibilities of pollution, social exploitation of poorer, arguably less educated, societies, and the like. Diffine (1982) argues that Capitalism contains its own built-in checks and balances. People are required to exercise sound judgment, or suffer the consequences of their own folly. Of course, the underlying assumption here is one of knowledge and expertise. Blame the poor for not improving themselves, yet make sure the doors to the institutions of higher learning are closed to all but the elite. A rather well-known colleague of mine was recently chided about the particular choice of university where he earned his PhD. The jab was, basically, that if he had been any good, why had he not earned his degree from one of the name-brand universities, like Harvard, or

Yale, or even NYU? My retort to the largely ignorant individual framing such an obtuse bloviation was that during the period in which the degree was sought by my colleague, almost all university doors were closed to this person; you see, my friend and colleague is a 70-year-old black American, and Meredith v. Mississippi had not yet occurred. Thus, it seems hardly reasonable to assert that "the consequences of our own folly" is the standard we really seek to support and enforce. Capitalism does not carry any guarantee, granted that. A man risks failure along with the prospect of success. In the words of Robert Frost, "...I want the cream to rise." Capitalism puts the responsibility where it belongs, according to Diffine, on the individual, which is the meaning of true economic independence. Capitalism, arguably, is the system of the working man; it does not reward the idle. The beginning of the entrepreneur's credo goes something like: "I do not choose to be a common man ...I seek opportunity ...I do not wish to be a kept citizen, humbled and dulled by having the state look after me ...this with God's help ..." Of course, all of this is silent regarding environmental issues like racism, segregation, Communism and such.

The counter-argument goes something more along the lines of needing the ability for informed consent. In certain circles, extortion or coercion is criminal behavior. Yet when applied to other contextual environments, it is simply a part of doing business. For example, the choice of workers in a small village in Africa may well be starvation or accepting work for inherently "slave wages" by a firm that will exploit this low-cost labor into huge profits for shareholders. This is indeed the SWM model. And while the ethical judgments are wide and varying, at the end of the day, the outcomes are in clear conflict with Christian tradition and teachings. Even Luther would lose this argument.

The bottom line is that Capitalism is based on practices prohibited by the Bible for 1,500 years. Capitalism, without the tricks of putting on appropriate social masks, magnifies the arguably grotesque gap between the rich and poor. Theologically, Capitalism is inconsistent with the teachings and example of Jesus and is opposed to the Gospels and basic tenets of Christianity. Capitalism as a system is dependent on consumerism, and is therefore highly destructive to spiritual values. Ideally, we, as an 85% Christian society, must work towards a system, a hybrid perhaps, which balances the proven incentives of Capitalism and the compassion and justice of Socialism. Today, we seek our spiritual satisfaction and our ego satisfaction in consumption. This is clearly a relationship antithetical to Christ's teachings.

When the U.S. government talks about promoting democracy around the world, what it really means, most often, is the promotion of Capitalism. George Carlin's somewhat cynical tirade of the 1970s spoke of "laying a little Capitalism on them ...U.S. Capitalism ..." Even China now gets Normal Trade Relations (formerly Most Favored Nation) status, because it allowed our corporations to come in and profit from the sale of Chinese goods (often made by slave labor and child labor) to Americans and others. It is the very Wal- Mart example of self-interest by consumers. Would you rather pay
$40.00 for a shovel made in a union shop here in the U.S.A., or $11.00 for a comparable shovel made by child labor in China? I am slightly embarrassed and a bit dismayed, again, to say give me the $11.00 shovel. But I am confident I am not alone. (Comfort in numbers.)

An interesting statistic about wealth distribution is as follows: The net assets of the 400 richest Americans are $300 billion, while the total net assets of the 150 million poorest Americans are zero. According to Dr. Robert Shutz, if just the unearned income of these rich were redistributed, every adult in America could be given $30,000 a year. More statistics show that in 1970, the richest 1% of Americans owned 20% of the nation's wealth. By 1989, it was 40%, and today it is more like 60–70%. The aggregate, broad-based standard of living in this country is declining rapidly.

And in a soon-to-be-released book, also written by the author, titled *Shantytown*, the economic impact of this decline in the standard of living is described in graphic terms of a newly emerging third-world nation: The U.S.A. All too often both husband and wife must work, and many often have two and three jobs, without benefits or retirement plans. Is Capitalism working? So much for the "pragmatism" spoken of as a reality of Capitalism. It may be working for the wealthy few, but certainly not for the many. The religious metaphor of the image of God urges business to be responsible ethically and communally to society, and individually within the structures of Capitalism in general, and of corporations in particular. It seems as though such is no longer the case, if it ever was. Former Fed Chairman Alan Greenspan spoke about "infectious greed" with regard to American corporate leadership. He noted that while rank and file wages have increased by 36% over the last decade, the wage percentage increase for chief executive officers rose 340%. When a CEO can clear $1 billion during his or her tenure, clearly executive pay is too high. Now, Jesus taught that we would be judged by how we treat the least of our brothers and sisters. And even Peter Drucker argued in the 1980s that no leader should make more than twenty times the lowest-paid employee. Perhaps the methodology includes starting to evaluate business leaders by what they do for everyone involved in their enterprise

(Welch, 2003).

"I have been born again according to John 3:3 and I pledge to hold the highest Biblical code of ethics in my business transactions ...we can make no warranty of any kind with regard to the services or products of the advertisers herein" (Swomley, 1996, p. 39). This was published in a Christian business directory. The dichotomy is obvious. This illustrates, if not is, the very essence of what must be changed. We just cannot continue to try to have it both ways. We either support a Biblical perspective on business or a Capitalist one, but we cannot continue to serve two masters.

Recently, a Christian organization made a decision regarding its hiring policies. In a secular part of its business model, the company implemented and incorporated a sort of Christian mandate to a formerly secular aspect of the model. The explanation was simply, "If we didn't add this, than we might have to hire someone who is a non- Christian. This way, we can mandate only Christians may apply." It seems there is at least an ethical inconsistency here.

XI._Calvin Got It Wrong

In 1904, sociologist Max Weber published *The Protestant Ethic and The Spirit of Capitalism*. He argued that the Reformation vis-à-vis the several new Protestant religions was the precondition of the growth of modern Capitalism. He referred to the concept of "calling" in Calvinism, it being held that God should be worshipped through work and that worldly enterprises were satisfying to God. This, of course, was from a man whose basic faith tenet was one of Biblical and dogmatic mandate v. good works. After all of the turmoil in the split of the early church, in that the Catholics pursued a "works"-based gospel and sold indulgences for the construction of St. Peter's Basilica in Rome, these were significant and obviously very meaningful, and it seems a bit disingenuous, if not absurd, to find Calvin supporting a "works"-based ethic not frowned upon by God. Further, he argued that God would bestow worldly success on the "saved." Imagine, earthly rewards for divinely inspired behavior ...hmmm.

Weber suggested that this pulled together with the idea of an "elect" who would be ultimately "saved." This is the Harold Camping argument—one of many, actually, which have included projections about the end of the world, the coming rapture and, most recently, the end of the church age. This, Weber argued, was what drove Capitalism in the 19th century. Pre-Reformation, Catholicism was opposed to profit, and especially usury (the lending of money for profit without risk). These sentiments are also found in the context of the Koran—an older perspective, perhaps. But in 1515, theologian Johann Eck came up with a way around the usury problem: He devised a system of contracts whereby the borrower and the lender entered into a partnership in a particular venture. A profit was estimated, and the borrower sold the investment opportunity back to the lender for a profit smaller than the original estimate. The intent here should be obvious. Clearly the weasel wording is not what the Christian mandate contemplated. I just cannot see Jesus weasel-wording a perspective on the sellers (merchants) lined up outside the temple, selling their goods, any more than I can see Jesus being the head of a loan-sharking organization, lending money at a high rate of interest for the sake of earning interest. Phrase it or parse it any way you would like, but to borrow a phrase, "this dog don't hunt!"

An uncle of mine used to sneak away for weekends in Las Vegas with a friend of his whose last name was "Smith" (name changed to protect the parties.) When his wife asked where he was going, and with whom, he said Atlantic City with Smith. Of course, the wife assumed it was Mr. Smith, not Mrs. Smith. Here, again, the intent is obvious. Was this technically a Christian doing by virtue of the legalistic correctness of the answers to the questions asked? Well, then, I propose the same argument in the face of this so-called "Protestant work ethic."

These aforementioned and other dealings led Martin Luther (1483–1546), one of the instigators of the Reformation, to challenge that the Catholic Church was too involved in the worldly activity of making money. The church was too interwoven, arguably, with "profit and Capitalist motives" in the building of St. Peter's and other financial contrivances — this, of course, ostensibly the basis for the break. This was another one of those dichotomous behaviors that pitted Luther against the concept in terms of the Catholic Church, but one that he and Calvin defended, which led to an atmosphere in which the pursuit of wealth could seemingly go unhindered. Weber described the resultant Capitalism as one of the "glories of Protestantism." In fact, the so-called "Protestant work ethic" was the result of Calvinism and Methodism …specifically dealing with the mining and industrial towns of England at the end of the 18th century, whereby Methodism encouraged its followers to become methodic and sober, the reward for which would be delivered in the next world. It created the disciplined workforce needed to insure capitalistic success in the market place.

Thus we can see the seemingly self-serving, albeit Capitalist, tendencies that were heavily promoted by the Protestant factions of the time, towards the end of providing and preserving the newly adopted Capitalist mentality. The end game was the creation of surplus, by this disciplined approach to hard work, and frugal living.

Nowadays, evangelical Christians take this Protestant work ethic a step further by surmising that any increase in material wealth can be equated to God's blessing for their efforts; kind of like greed and wealth—or excess, if you will—being sanctioned by God because of the rightness and good job they have done. Being labeled as somewhat religious zealots by some, it did not take long, according to Alex Paterson (2003), for significant numbers of evangelicals to rationalize that "the end justifies the means" in their seemingly ruthless pursuit of wealth. The result of this ethos today is American Capitalism and, coincidentally, American Evangelicalism. Lately, it seems hard to distinguish between the two. The differences between Joel Osteen and Bill Gates are largely product related and based on a few zeros in terms of gross revenue; the same between AT&T and
T.D. Jakes. You get my point.

This ethos today is magnified and somewhat glorified in movies like *Wall Street*, where Gordon Gekko, the character played by Michael Douglas, proffers that "greed is good." But to be sure, this behavior, as much as the behavior espoused by Calvin, is a perversion, if not outright contradiction of the behaviors espoused by Jesus and written of in the Bible. The Jesus-born concepts of "think of others before thyself" and "do unto others as you would have them do unto thyself" all present the basic issues of the dilemma before the altars of Capitalism and Christianity. Christians—who comprise over 85% of the American population, according to polling conducted around the last presidential election—have largely convinced themselves, according to Paterson, that the "relentless pursuit of material wealth is their God given right, if not duty" (2003). This is illustrated, perhaps painfully, but reasonably, by the mega- televangelists who prod millions out of their congregations in exchange for "salvation" in a very overt and, arguably, degrading example of the perversion of the words and mission of Jesus. An argument that did not work against the Catholics from their critics for the sale of "indulgences" in the building of Saint Peter's Basilica in Rome is equally unlikely to work in the Protestant Evangelical argument of the Crystal Cathedral or Brooklyn Tabernacle. Perhaps the more common perspective, albeit somewhat cynical, is found in how polite Americans seem to be to each other as they rip each other off and stab each other in the back, all in the name of competition (Paterson, 2003).

Well, it is not too far a stretch to relate that same argument to the ethic applied by the haves against the have-nots, be they ordained clergy or not. And if you stop to think about it, the maintenance of such a system requires a large pool of ill-informed, naïve people to feed upon themselves; alas, the ordained would not be so likely to be able to "pull it off"! Per Paterson, this pool of stupidity is maintained by a public education system that is clearly existing within a culture of crass materialism and continually reinforced by television, expressing dumbed-down views and ethics aimed at the lowest common denominator; sheep to the slaughter, to be sure. The fox in the henhouse is not an analogy that is overtly misapplied when referencing the "shepherd and the sheep."

Evangelical Christianity today has a significant influence on how Americans think and behave towards each other and the rest of the world. Evangelical Christianity did not invent "private enterprise" nor "Capitalism," but the organization's wholehearted support of the more corrupt aspects of the same legitimizes those traits and, in turn, defines what is considered acceptable behavior by the nation as a whole (Paterson, 2003).

A friend was recently called back to work at a Christian College in New York City, after the accreditation of the college was pulled for a variety of reasons, many surrounding the lack of transparency and integrity in the academic process, awarding of grades, adherence to Federal Financial Aid guidelines, and more. In the minds of some, the college became a "cash cow" of sorts, pulling in many dollars to be used for the Christian agenda of the organization, delivering a marginal product at the end of the day—and this is to be viewed as moral and ethical? It is without question "an end justifies the means" argument, whereby and wherein the institution at large pursues its greater agenda with less regard for and deference to the vehicle being used to generate the revenue for same. One has to wonder whether Jesus would have thought this an appropriate methodology in furtherance of the mission—His mission!

The original idea, which was, arguably, perverted by Calvin, was the calling of all lay people and clergy to penetrate the structures of society and influence them from within. This is the same argument being perverted by many Christian colleges and other organizations, and for ostensibly the same agenda or purpose. It is an arguably rare instance when an organization like one of these has the ability to synthesize and integrate the value systems, the dichotomous value systems of both of these paradigms, Capitalism and Christianity, and attempt to resolve these into a holistic and fully integrated worldview. This endeavor is, at least for the moment, being considered if not pursued by at least one Christian college, with a business school: Nyack College. And while it seems that the integration of these paradigms is easier on some days than others, and while the tension between the "Evangelical Right" and the "Dark Side" (the business side) exists, to be sure, the tension is thus far aimed at recognition in anticipation of solutions and resolutions. What outcomes will emerge is at the moment, uncertain.

This is what Jesus meant when he called his disciples to be salt and light in a world of decay and darkness (Matt. 5:13-6). A close friend, probably closer before I turned down his gracious offer of employment at a Christian College in Florida, Dr. Lyle Bowlin, is a shining example of what is spoken of in Matt. 5-13-6. Lyle is very much the strong advocate for moral and ethical perspective and behavior in a business world sometimes characterized as full of "decay and darkness." Lyle is decidedly the "salt and light" spoken of in Matthew and, to be even more direct, the very theme spoken of by the President of Southeastern College, Dr. Mark Rutland, in frequent lectures and homilies. Organizations like these with people like Dr. Bowlin represent what I would characterize as a last best hope for reconciliation, if not resolution, of these two seemingly dichotomous paradigms. Calvin believed that the work of priests was no more valued than the work of any other profession, in the eyes of God. He promoted that one's vocation is to serve God in whatever one pursues. This requires a reprogramming of thought as we attempt to apply Calvin's objectives in a sea of materialism, if we are to try to live as followers of Jesus Christ. If we claim to thirst for God, then we must break the dependency on the convenience of Calvin's words, and in crisis seek the true meaning of the Biblical perspective on how we are to relate to one another …and at the end of the day, it is not to be found in Western Capitalism (Tewell, 2003).

Bishop John Spong, arguably a maverick in many respects in his own right, suggests a call for a new Reformation—clearly a nonconforming idea in the eyes of many. However, I agree. In looking back to the Reformation, he argues that there was much doctrine upon which both sides agreed: The trinity, Jesus as the incarnate Son of God, the reality of heaven and hell, et. al. He argues that the divisions were largely trivial, in retrospect: for example, whether salvation was achieved by faith alone, as Luther argued, or whether faith without work was dead, as the Vatican quoted the Epistle of James. At the end of the day, the fight pitted Christians against Christians …it was a battle over issues of Church order, not core theological issues. Thus, in terms of outcomes, on aggregate, the church must, in Spong's words, abandon its reliance on guilt as a motivator of behavior and among other things, all human beings must be respected for what each is, bearing the image of God. This is a compelling argument. And while Spong is widely criticized in some circles for his arguably liberal views on gay marriage, homosexuality in general, some expressions in support of abortion and women in religious service capacities and such, his thoughts about integration, the sense of coming together—or, perhaps more poignantly put, the "politics of inclusion," to quote Jesse Jackson—are very much related to what Jesus would likely advocate in terms of behaviors …thus another dichotomy. Face it: All factions seem to have the Capitalism part down pat. It is the integration part that seems to be proving the difficulty.

Norman Council writes that the oldest still-surviving corporation is the Benedictine Order of the Catholic Church, established circa 529 A.D. He argues that long before Calvin was the church culture of proselytizing, which was interpreted to mean not just a right, but an outright duty to convert, to "civilize" lands overrun in this process. It was, in effect, the seminal beginnings, albeit under the pretext of colonial and economic imperialism, of what evolved into modern- day Western Capitalism. Council (2004) suggests that a Capitalism that continues to operate as if it is entitled to unrestricted dominion over the earth, will eventually destroy the substrate of its own existence.

XII._Theistic v. Vulture Capitalism

Without much argument, it seems as though where we draw lines—boundaries, if you will—becomes important. The proverbial "line in the sand" may well be the concoction or euphoric design of much organizational theory and, indeed, soft science analysis, but it seems true to the point in terms of analyzing precisely degrees or limitations. An argument I often use with my students includes discussion on the subject of intent. I would argue that intent is, in a real sense, everything! Intent certainly seems to me to be the crux of the issue at hand. Clearly, intent is the difference between manslaughter and murder, between conversion and theft by deception, and since intent is so contextual, one might extend the argument in terms of esoteric, if not just nuanced Capitalistic, intent as well. Is the purpose of the larger religious paradigms, the big cathedrals and congregations, a matter of money? Or is it really a more intrinsically valuable purpose that is sought? Is the preaching of "feel-good religion," the brand of

Joel Osteen, simply a product with a return, or is it truly about the mission and the Word? So what of intent? How to judge the heart of a person? Was engineering school too difficult so I went to seminary instead? Was Hollywood out of reach, so I took to the religious stage? Or is the decision related to true evangelism, truly spreading the word because of faith and a deeply held belief structure? And if the latter, then why the mansions? Why the fancy cars? The private jets? The $4,500 suits? Can I not spread the Word of Jesus without a new Corvette, without living in mansions, and with opulence beyond belief? And what of the Capitalist side of the equation? Maximize shareholder value? Corporate social responsibility?

To borrow from Moffett, as cited in earlier chapters, the difference between SWM and CWM is the difference between night and day and, by design, intent. A Western Capitalist model that apologizes not for taking advantage of an arguably liberal interpretation of "eminent domain" in taking generations-old family property to put up a shopping mall, of course for the greater economic good ...well, the shareholder attraction is clearly there. But would such a proposition succeed in the CWM paradigm of greater equity between stakeholder groups? Would, for example, Marubeni Corporation of Japan be so determined to take property from third- and fourth-generation Japanese elder citizens against their will for the economic benefit of the shareholders of the firm? I cannot be sure of that, but it seems doubtful to me. Is CWM more in tune with Christian behaviors?

Nomenclature ...Passive Capitalism? Vicious Capitalism? Theistic Capitalism? Vulture Capitalism? Perhaps the nomenclature that we apply is significant regarding the issue at hand; it reflects perhaps what we really think, or how we actually perceive the relationship between Capitalism and Christianity. It is certainly telling, in any event. While perhaps a bit nuanced, it does in fact speak to how we integrate specifically the behaviors arguably sought after. And yet relate those behaviors to a form of Capitalism that still resembles Capitalism?

An expression that comes to my mind to describe the Capitalism that Jesus might likely endorse could be construed as Theistic, or perhaps Humanistic Capitalism. Or maybe it is simply Theism and Humanism, after all. This idea of a softer, gentler Capitalism with a heart, where the tenets and precepts of the Bible and other religious traditions are followed and incorporated into the specific behaviors, the environments and corporate cultures—what kind of Capitalism would this be? For example, while working for the Japanese firm, there was an occasion where a business deal was structured; prices, materials and such agreed to; delivery and installation features identified and arrangements made satisfactorily to both parties. Upon delivery and installation, the production was going slower than anticipated and required by the end user. A somewhat traditional American response was usually "if you need more training, we can provide it at a cost." But the argument ensued that the equipment purchased was towards a particular end, and that end was not being satisfactorily met. In the high context and honorable social and cultural structure of the Japanese firm, more training was provided as necessary to effect the end that was originally contemplated and envisioned, at no further cost. This kind of deal, while seemingly foreign to some, in effect follows the tenets of Theistic or Humanistic Capitalism and their teachings (or what those teachings might be), and thus might be considered an example of Theistic or Humanistic Capitalism at work. And what did we really do? We followed the example of teachings that were neither contractually obligated, nor financially mandated. We did something we were not bound to do by "the rules."

The closest supportive argument in this Western Capitalist model is likely found in the Randy Pohlman value over time argument, subset in Value Driven Management. It speaks to many things, including the long-term perspective vs. the short-term quarter-to-quarter mentality of gains and value. But even this is wholly insufficient for resolving the bigger dilemma.

Of course, the other direction in this example would be the hard- hearted, typically

American approach reflective of a low-context society that suggests a deal is a deal, and the contract is everything. If it ain't in the contract, it does not exist. Thus the end user would be required to fund additional training costs and incidentals, and the contract provisions would be upheld. Would it be right? Would it be wrong? Well, it is not as much about right or wrong as it is about choice—the choice being how do you intend to conduct your business affairs? Here again, context and intent are everything. Is the intent of what was discussed and contemplated in putting the deal together at its inception superior to the contract language to which weeks, likely months, of discussions were reduced? Or is the "honorable" thing to do to behave in a way supportive of the reliance placed on the good will and good intentions of the parties paramount? The choice to adhere to the strict contract language, while seemingly good business, is certainly reminiscent of a type of Vulture Capitalism. This hard-lined approach, which says *we're entitled to every nickel we're entitled to, and it says so right here*, is exactly what this Western Capitalist model has degenerated into. Of course, the terms employed are more akin to "efficiency," "maximization of utility," "contractual certainties," and such. Let's call it what it is: Vulture Capitalism. As to which, in the words of Dr. David Schroeder, might be considered "Christ-Like Behavior"? I think the choice is obvious.

XIII._Conclusion

In a recent work, Stratis (2004) cites Chewning, who argues that there is a real need in many Christian colleges for professors who can integrate ethics, faith and business. It is certainly significant and widely held that change must evolve from inside organizations and structures and, as such, perhaps the seminal chain proposed by Chewning has merit. If the professors, the inspirers of students and of the next generation of managers, can influence change in the minds of future leaders, then the future leaders can effect this change and, ultimately, the nature of the Capitalist models integrated into the business paradigm going forward. Subsequently, behaviors, both business and liturgical, may be altered. Yet as just spoken of, if the purpose is the same Calvinist approach and exercise in *justification ethics*, this proposition is then likely doomed to fail. The duality of thought that lies at the crossing of the confusions— arguably, misinterpretations—by Calvin and supported by many factions of the Evangelical Christian mainstream must be embraced and resolved if we are to ever begin to resolve the differences that are so seminal in nature as to seem utterly irreconcilable, from where they lie today. If, indeed, the Bible is to be viewed and accepted as the inspired word of God, this concept in itself is the subject of huge debate, not the least part of which surrounds Gnostic Gospels and writings, the Apocrypha, and such. Somewhat self-servingly perhaps, those books were simply "written out" of the Bible instead of being included. If in fact such things as the Trinity exist, in the forms suborned by Christians, along with other dogmatic aspects of belief, then the Bible must be found to support those ideals of human equality and condition that have been peppered throughout this paper, and characterized as Christ-like behaviors. If, in fact, 85% of our society is truly Christian, then I fail to see the problem in implementation, excepting, of course, that there is no one definitive interpretation and understanding of the Bible. Christianity, its very nature, the Bible, historical or liturgical and, of course, which Bible and books are we speaking of precisely all factor in. Further, there are other significant problems, as we again are very kind to ourselves in terms of our Christian identities, and such. Christ-like behavior, for example, as Dave Schroeder puts it, must be the rule of the day; the underlying patterns of how we relate and treat our fellow beings, society, and all of the behaviorally driven elements of being. Decency towards other human beings, while abstract, certainly is not so difficult to understand; an arguably more equitable distribution of the resources provided ultimately by the Creator, from which all things derive, and are ultimately consumed or otherwise acquired, is not so difficult to embrace, either. A recognition of individual achievement, but against that backdrop of a sincere desire to "move the humanist ball forward," albeit in small increments at times, but towards an end of a betterment of the aggregate human condition; but all for the ultimate glorification of the Creator. This is the Theistic, perhaps Humanistic Capitalism that must be embraced to begin to at least attempt to bridge the huge crevasse and dichotomy between Christianity and certainly this Western, much Americanized version of Capitalism that we enjoy.

But how likely is any of this? Even in the very futuristic writings of Feredoun Esfandiary, later renamed FM2030, where he speaks of a sort of John Lennon future wherein there is one world, one structure of accountability and responsibility beyond the pale of governments, national interests, flags and banners, religious segregations (distinctions, if you prefer), and where tools of the aggregate economy, like technological advancement, are legitimately used for the betterment of the human condition, the baseline argument is that this should somehow become the ultimate goal or purpose; or perhaps already is to some degree. But how then does this reconcile with Western Capitalism? Marxism! Socialism! Communism! I hear your screams. I can hear the echoes in the halls of Wall Street ...I can see the Andrew Carnegies spinning in their graves ...yet, just how different, but for the product or service, is Andrew Carnegie from, let's say, Joel Osteen? Hmmm ...Again, are we after something not achievable? Chewning would argue in opposition.

There seems to be almost more agreement or commonality of behavior between an extreme non-denominational futurist and Christ than Capitalism and Christ. FM2030, himself raised Muslim in a Muslim nation (Iran), shared more in common with the intended outcomes of Christian behavior, perhaps inspired by the Koran and the Imams of his youth, than the behaviors exhibited by a Capitalist nation purportedly 85% Christian. Can a nation of seemingly non- Christian behaviors, which is 85% Christian, truly be called a Christian nation? This perhaps can be the basis for the structural change proposed between Theistic and Vulture Capitalism. Is it as simple and intuitive as "act who you are"? Can it really be that being true to ourselves brings about the sought-after changes? While there is little debate in the ideal of life's purpose being that of continuity— in other words, to survive—there is a compelling and continuing argument as to the condition and methodologies used to accomplish this end. It would indeed be counterintuitive to propose that money or wealth is not related to this condition of survival. The fact that the Bible is silent—most certainly in the New Testament—

regarding an acceptable prescription for the accumulation and use of wealth, leaves little but the intent, as delineated in the Epistles, Gospels and other teachings bulwarked by the Bible, including portions of the Old Testament. And again these, being so highly interpretive and contextual in application, and of course selective by design in terms of which books and what writings actually "made the final cut" in the Bible, lend little to the resolution of the aggregate dilemma. Moreover, since there must obviously be change, and it is unlikely that the faith-based belief structures of Christianity, by definition, are likely to or will even consider change as a sort of dogmatic pragmatic progression, the moving entity here is by force of reduction: Then, Capitalism. Can this, in fact, be the moving entity? Could there be a poor Bill Gates? Could there be a purely altruistic Vanderbilt or John Astor? Could there be a poorly clothed T.D. Jakes? Would Joel Osteen take the A Train in lieu of the Benz? Who gets to give to the poor, and under what names? Are foundations for giving doomed to forfeit their assets to a central government that then redistributes them in the name of the sponsors? Politicians, not patricians? Hmmm ...

While, clearly, authors of secular texts, like Stonehill and Moffett, suggest varying denominations of Capitalism in terms of behavioral divisions like Shareholder Wealth Maximization, or simply shareholder-based models, and Corporate Wealth Maximization or corporation-based models, the latter of which position themselves as more "socially friendly," at the end of the day, there is a seemingly unbridgeable gap that indicates what is already and really quite intuitively apparent: Namely, that Capitalism and Christianity are and likely always will be mutually exclusive of each other; at least in their current forms and contexts.

Or are we to conclude that the seemingly varying models of Capitalism are much akin to the "denominational differences" of the varying movements within or under the Christian umbrella, wherein these two paradigms cannot comfortably coexist in the absence of real structural change, how, who, where and when? And while different models and, subsequently, different rhetoric, labels and nomenclature attempt to provide at least a rhetorical bridge or hiatus between Capitalism and Christianity, whence will come the structural changes?

Yet these are two major paradigms and differences, or resultant "shifts," that have attempted to ameliorate the stigma of pure greed- oriented Capitalism and have thus far been largely unsuccessful window-dressing. Needless to say, not much has changed dogmatically on the part of the other paradigm, either. The brand of Capitalism upon which Western society has largely been built is just not a very Christian paradigm, it seems, as a matter of fact, it is pure Vulture Capitalism, Darwinian in design. And while again both intent and context are important, the thought process that puts forth "kinder and gentler" Capitalist tendencies cannot be sustained in an argument surrounding business purpose in its present form, its present environment, its present leadership structure and its present lack of recognition and vision towards meaningful change. The counter-argument or, in a sense, duality of purpose espoused by the more seemingly even-keeled position of Asian Capitalism, as an example, a distinction raised by Michael Moffett, suggests a less harsh "greed element" in the structure itself; again, less vulture-like, supported in its entirety by an almost Theistic-like application of reasonableness and what some might call Christ-like behavior. While perhaps not necessarily referred to in that exact way, there lies a seemingly closer relationship between Asian Capitalism and Christian behaviors than there does in an arguably more Christian nation.

Perhaps this is reflected best, or at least well, in the comparative analysis of CEO pay scales in Eastern vs. Western Capitalist business communities. It has often, albeit somewhat anecdotally, been pointed out that American CEOs make tens if not hundreds of times more than their Asian counterparts. And without exception, these same articles recognize no major gap in talent or abilities as an explanation for such significant and vast differences in overall compensation. But then a Capitalism that speaks of socially responsible and warm and friendly is not, at the end of the day, a model of Western Capitalism, or corporate governance that supports it as we know and recognize it. Christianity that speaks of equal treatment even for the lowest among us ultimately cannot abdicate that position for one of individual profit and personal gain.

Basically, then, a tiger does not change its stripes, and the tiger of Capitalism in its current forms can likely never be a vehicle that would serve the purposes of Jesus. And the 900-pound gorilla of Christianity in the living room of business, to which few are speaking, can never be a small and unnoticeable way of simply trying to make more ethical Capitalists of Capitalists. I mean, what would the objective be: to make a more ethical greedy bastard? To add an ethos of care and concern as we turn out widows and orphans onto the streets of America to make way for new development under the guise of "eminent domain"? This is what is embodied in "render unto Caesar, and unto God ..." These are two separate and distinct animals. A dog cannot fly, and a bird cannot bark. Christ could never advocate a purely Capitalist ethos, and Capitalists could never support a truly socialist, arguably Christian ethos or agenda. A paradigm shift of the highest order is mandated to this end, but seems most unlikely.

Having said all this, there is, akin to a pebble's ripple in the otherwise clear and calm pond of business and Capitalist retrospective,

Dr. Randy Pohlman's Value-Driven Management, where he speaks of the value over time proposition. The intended, or perhaps it is unintended, consequence of this value over time proposition is a seemingly kinder and gentler hiatus between this value proposition and how it plays out between the entities. And while at times from the most unlikely of sources, in his "value funnel," he integrates the major elements of the macro-environment, as well as the various stakeholder groups often addressed in the CWM model, spoken of earlier. He distills business performance down to sales, profits, market share, image, net present value, and value over time, which feeds back into the value funnel. Of importance, however, is the proposition that seems to at least attempt to wrestle with the SWM v. CWM models of capitalistic behavior, in terms of addressing some of the groups of interest vis-à-vis the behavior propositions put forth in Matthew 5 and Luke 6; put forth in Pohlman's eight facets. An argument as to how compelling or not, I suspect, is the very crux of the issue, and suggests that a possible hiatus or bridge between Capitalism and Christianity may, in fact, at least to a degree, be found in the value over time proposition by Pohlman. Of course, the prospects of an environment similar to that espoused by FM2030 are an alternative as well. In effect, he also reduces the rancor and acidity and even the significance of the perspective of pure shareholder self-interest into the proposition that decisions that affect the longer term may provide the true value in the value proposition, without regard to border, flag, ancestry, etc. And while still being consistent in terms of purpose, but yet beginning to at least address the interests of the heretofore disenfranchised other stakeholder groups, many of which were the historical constituencies of Jesus, it provides an opening. It is a place to start, for Christian university professors and students.

In the alternative, however, the value proposition of Pohlman only begins to address the issues at the heart of the debate over Capitalist behaviors, hence little in terms of outcomes. There is no firm or committed determination as to the specific behaviors or remedies mandated by Christian conscience, if not dogma (again, as most of the Bible is silent regarding specific solutions). John Paul II, in a recent encyclical before he died, warned of the dangers of unbridled greed. One might argue that Pohlman sets the stage for "improved" SWM behaviors, albeit in a more secular form, and others might, of course, argue the contra position, that being it does little beyond the effective CWM acknowledgement, and only then tangentially, regarding addressing any proposition of change.

John Kay, Director of Oxford University's New School of Management Studies, in an interview with *Fortune* magazine, addressed the very issue of wealth maximization. In effect, Kay suggested that managers today seem to work to balance interests as well as interest groups, incorporating the very stakeholders addressed in Moffett's CWM model. Pohlman suggests that the false dichotomy of cornering Capitalist business into one of two corners, social welfare or shareholder wealth, is incorrect in that "the real world is far more complicated and interconnected." And while again a noteworthy point, the distinctives of the SWM and CWM models cannot simply be brushed aside as a matter of convenience. These are core issues. These are cornerstone issues of structure, and faith and belief. And further, while seemingly rigid and obviously polarized, the crevasse between the two Capitalist models is the very distinctive of each system, all of which likely leads us back to this bi-modal perspective of which Pohlman speaks.

Indeed, in viewing the two models and transposing history, one might logically conclude that were the models reversed, the Asian dominance of the 1980s might never have occurred, but then the innovations domestically of the last one hundred years might have occurred in another geographical location entirely. Might it be "Mike" Nakamura in lieu of Michael Jordan, or perhaps "Chris" Tsuji in lieu of Chris Everett—one can only imagine. Perhaps the papers would be full of stories about Tetsuzo Bonds in lieu of Barry Bonds, "Donald" Miazaki in lieu of Donald Trump, Amelia Chong in lieu of

Amelia Earhart ...the alternative possibilities are virtually endless.

Of course, the reality is that there are firm boundaries to some things, and likely by definition, the varying brands of Capitalism are what they are. Thus forays into the arena of pure speculation—or Monday morning quarterbacking—are frivolous and non-productive flights of fantasy. By definition, John Kay is attempting to make Capitalism okay, in the true spirit of political correctness. Much akin to "congress person" vs. "congressman," "fireperson" vs. "fireman," in essence the remnants of Gloria Steinem, Shareholder Wealth Maximization theory is harsh, polarizing if not polarized, and largely politically incorrect in a society that seeks to marginalize, mitigate and otherwise create mediocrity out of individualism, independence and the absolute polarity of clear-cut definition; such definition as Western Capitalism with shareholder wealth as its prime directive. Again, as spoken of earlier, this "kinder and gentler" form of Capitalism is in the minds of those who least understand business purpose and the implications of economic change implicit in same. "Is America Number One" is a foray into economic freedom, by John Stossel of ABC. In an interview for a segment with Nobel Prize-winning economist Milton Friedman, the point is made quite directly that among the implications of a strong social policy, as in France and Germany, is included higher unemployment, less innovation or innovativeness, greater stagnation in terms of entrepreneurship. The resultant "brain drain" deprives the aggregate national structures of some of the brilliant thought that seeks to overcome and succeed and, inevitably, prosper. Societies are compared and contrasted in terms of highly centralized and de-centralized systems of both government and economic distribution, citing the successes of Hong Kong vs. some poorer sections of India, for example. The U.S.A., Australia, and the abject failures of certain sections of India, China and the pre- Perestroika U.S.S.R. are explored in some detail or, in other cases, simply alluded to. Friedman emphasizes the significant growth experienced in Hong Kong since the 1950s, and the fact that the innovativeness or entrepreneurial leadership exhibited, calling it "economic freedom," is the root cause. But this so-called economic freedom resembles virtually completely this Western Capitalist model. Comparative analysis highlights the similarities between Christian purpose and socialized societies, vs. the hard line innovativeness and overwhelming economic success of strongly Capitalist societies like Hong Kong, the U.S.A., etc. While perhaps intuitively bi-modal, at a minimum the conclusion infers the free enterprise, Capitalist model as being one of great potential and success. The lethargic and arguably debilitating nature of more socialized systems leads to the conclusion that while well intentioned, the more "social" views have significant consequences, some of which, while unintended, are the cause and effect and proximal result of failure. Even Friedman states that "nothing does more harm than good intentions," and juxtaposes this against the backdrop of the great "brain drain" cited by Stossel in examples including Andy Bechtelstein of Sun Microsystems, and others like Martine Kempf, who left their more socialist homelands in search of greater entrepreneurial opportunity. The irony, of course, inescapable as it is, is that the good done and created by the entrepreneurial efforts of these individuals in this Capitalist system arguably exceeds the alleged harshness of the Capitalist system itself.

There is a corollary to "tough love" here that needs mentioning. Sometimes, the "spare the rod, spoil the child" perspective holds value, even today in what some might argue to be a very "liberal" child-rearing environment, where discipline is lacking. Could it be that Capitalism is the discipline that provides the harshness and structure to create greater good for society at large? Is the extreme wealth distribution pattern simply a reflection of an economic "daddy," applying a social "rod" of sorts? Perhaps what seems so Darwinian at first glance is simply the Christian imperative of "tough love." Is this the hiatus between the two paradigms?

Ultimately, the politicians and the clerics will continue to interpret and re-interpret both

Capitalism and the Bible, and apply them in very convenient fashion to the arguments being juxtaposed at the time. But by definition, Capitalism is neither gentle nor "fair." Christianity is neither about wealth accumulation nor exploitation, nor is it entrepreneurial. These two dichotomous paradigms are much akin to the often-claimed right among friends: That of being able to disagree and remain friends.

Thus, it seems they are and shall forever remain separate and distinct, unless the harsh brand of Vulture Capitalism yields and morphs into something other than its current harsh self. A new system must be devised from the inside, using the influences in part suggested by Chewning, in order to achieve the common goals of mankind: To alleviate suffering, to bridge the wealth/poverty crevasse, and to address the basic nature of incentive, yet find those elements that foster cooperation. A synergistic system that looks to the utopian outcomes sought after in the 1960s, but applies the harsh, sometimes Darwinian efforts of this shareholder-driven model, has been sought, arguably, since time before Christ. This will take, at a minimum, synthesis of thought, intent, capital, political will and, at bottom, the modern manifestation of the essence of Matthew 5 and Luke 6, and the behaviors espoused within the context of those passages. Behavior change! What a novel idea! Perhaps FM2030 had it right after all. Perhaps all the things that divide peoples and societies are the things that need to disappear first. John Lennon spoke of no hell or heaven, no governments—in essence, no source of divisions, or divisiveness.

As with any journey or endeavor ever undertaken, a starting point, a place to begin, may be found in the essence of the behaviors spoken of in Matthew 5 and Luke 6. For at the end of the day, it is the actions or behaviors that will produce the results ...as in the words of Milton Friedman, nothing does so much harm as good intentions. Actions
...arguably the works side of the gospel, which espouses faith and works, is perhaps the truest intent of how we are to conduct our lives in the face of the Capitalist and Christian dichotomy. Perhaps actions do indeed speak louder than words.

Certainly, much more work is in order as a precursor to any effort to resolve or sufficiently address this dilemma. And while the Joel Osteens and T.D. Jakes and Robert Schullers of the world continue to preach their words of God in the face of ever-increasing personal materialism and wealth, the incongruity of their message need only be obviated by a trip to Kenya, or India or China, where the human condition can be seen for what represents the worst in Capitalism: Namely, the neglect and lack of social compassion for those the weakest among us.

In *The Prophet*, Gibran writes, "And a merchant said, Speak to us of Buying and Selling. And he answered and said: To you the earth yields her fruit, and you shall not want if you but know how to fill your hands. It is in exchanging the gifts of the earth that you shall find abundance and be satisfied. Yet unless the exchange be in love and kindly justice, it will but lead some to greed and others to hunger." And he concludes by saying, "For the master spirit of the earth shall not sleep peacefully upon the wind till the needs of the least of you are satisfied."

Thus, it is counter-intuitive to believe that one can acquire riches, wear the finest clothes, drive the fastest, most expensive cars, and eat at the finest restaurants while, just out of eyeshot, in abject poverty, a child's mouth goes unfilled, a stomach endures the hunger pangs of emptiness, and the spirit of despair abounds. This is not and cannot be a party to the Christian paradigm. Clearly, one may be a Capitalist or a Christian, but not both; or one may entertain change and bridge the gap. Theistic or Humanistic Capitalism or Vulture Capitalism: which shall we embrace? A question for the ages? A question for our times!

BIBLIOGRAPHY

52148: The West: Capitalism, Progress and Christianity. (2004, January). Study Guide, Central Queensland University.

Acharya, S. (2001). The Origins of Christianity and the Quest for the Historical Jesus Christ. Truth Be Known. http://www.truthbeknown.com/origins.htm

Agle, B.R. (1998, March). Make a Difference in the World. *Business and Society*, 37(1), 102–103.

Bachelder, R. (1990, December). Capitalism and Christianity: Pulling on Both Oars. *The Christian Century*, 1194–1197.

Bandow, D. (2000, May). God and the Economy: Is Capitalism Moral? *Freedom Daily*. http://www.fff.org.freedom/0500e.asp

Bennett, John. (1946). Christian Ethics and Social Policy Blinder, Alan. (1987).

American Economics Review 77, (2), 130-36.

Bowman, R. M. (2004a, January). Brief History of Christianity and Capitalism. http://www.rmbowman.com/catholic/econom2.htm

Bowman, R.M. (2004b, January). Capitalism and Democracy. http://www.rmbowman.com/catolic/econom6.htm

Bowman, R.M. (2004c, January). Is Capitalism Working Today? http://www.rmbowman.com/catholic/econom4.htm

Bragg, J. (2002, November). Q&A on the Ethics of Christianity v. Capitalism. *The Daily Journal of Capitalism*. http://www.moraldefense.com/Initium/11-03-02.htm

Campbell, Joseph. (1997). The Power of Myth with Bill Moyers. http://www.mysticfire.com/

Christianity, Socialism, and Capitalism. (2004, Jan Christian Parents. http://www.christianparents.com/social2.htm Council, N. (2004, Summer). Christianity, Capitalism, Corporations, and the Myth of Dominion. Double Standards. http://www.doublestandards.org/council1.html 10/21/2005

Cronk, R. (1996). Ethics in America in the Wake of Christianity. Art on the Rebound: A Collection of Essays by R. Cronk. http://www.westland.net/venice/art/cronk/ethics.htm

Diffine, D.P. (1982,December/January). Friends or Foes? *Biblical Economics Today*, 4(6), F-6–F-9.

Doti, J. (1982). Capitalism and Greed. http:// www.earlyclassicalliberalism/cap…

Drucker, Peter F. (1999, June 1). The Rise and return of Pluralism. Wall Street Journal.

FM 2030. Are You a Transhuman, (January, 1989). Warner Books.

Giacalone, R.A & Jurkiewicz, C.L. (2003, August). Right from Wrong: The Influence of Spirituality on Perceptions of Unethical Business Activities. *Journal of Business Ethics*, 46(1), 85.

Gibran, K. (1968). The Prophet

Gladden, Washington. (1876). Working People and Their Employees. [Publisher unknown]

Goldman, E. (1913, April). The Failure of Christianity. Positive Atheism. http://www.positiveatheism.org/hist/goldman413.htm

Hacker, Jacob. (2002). The Divided Welfare State: The Battle over public and private social benefits in the United States. Cambridge University Press.

Hanciles, J. J. (2003, October). Migration and Mission: Some Implications for the Twenty-First-Century Church. *International Bulletin of Missionary Research*, 27(4), 146–153.

Hardaway, B. Christianity and Capitalism, Part Foundational Issues. Tektonics. http://www.tektonics.org/bhcap01.html

Harries, Richard. (1992). Is there a gospel for the rich? Mowbray Publications.

Hauerwas, Stanley. (December, 1984). The Peaceable Kingdom: A primer in Christian ethics. University of Notre Dame Press.

Huntington, S.P. (1996). The Clash of the Civilizations and Remaking of World Order. Simon Schuster, London, UK.

Laski, J. Shantytown (un-published manuscript) [2005] Latourette, K.S. (1947). Journal of Modern History, VOL. 19, Pg 54. University of Chicago Press.

Lee, E. (1993). Three Myths of Christianity: Morality vs. Ethics. Truth Seeker. http://www.truthseeker.com/truth-seeker/1993archive/120_6/ts206m.html

Lee, K.H., McCann, D.P., and Ching, M.A. (2003, March). Christ and Business Culture: A Study of Christian Executives in Hong Kong. *Journal of Business Ethics, 43*(1/2), 103–110.

Magill, G. (1992, February). Theology in Business Ethics: Appealing to the Religious Imagination. *Journal of Business Ethics, 11*(2), 129.

McCarraher, E. (2002, October). God: Half-off. *Commonweal, 129* (18), 22–24.

Mercieca, C. How Capitalism Undermines Christianity and Destroys Every Other Religion. International Association of Educators for World Peace. http://www.earthportals.com/Portal_Messenger/mercieca2.html

Mills, C. Wright. (1956). The Power Elite,

Oxford Press, New York. Moffett, M., Stonehill, A. and Eiteman, D.K. (2004). Multinational Business Finance, Pearson Publishing, New York.

Moll, R. (2003, November). Compassionate Capitalism. *Christianity Today.*

Moore, J. S. (2000). Plato, Christianity and World Politics.

Munby, D.L. (1961). God and the Rich Society: A study of Christians in a world of...Oxford University Press.

Nietzsche, Friedrich. (1965). The Portable Nietzsche, Viking Press, New York

Orwell, George. (2003). The Complete Works. http://www.george-orwell.org/

Origins of Christianity. (2005, October). http://www.holysmoke.org/hs00/xianity.htm

Paterson, A. (2003, October). Evangelical Christianity and Its Role in American Capitalism. http://www.vision.net.au/apaterson/social/evangeli.htm

Pohlman, R. and G.S. Gardiner. (2000). Value Driven Management. Amacom, New York, Boston.

Reichley, A.J. (1986). Theology Today. Religion in American Public Life.

Reuchlin, Abelard. True Authorship of the New Testament. http://www.holysmoke.org/hs00/xianity.htm

Rossouw, G. J. (1994, July). Business Ethics: Where Have All the Christians Gone? *Journal of Business Ethics, 13*(7), 557.

Sanders, James. (2006). Celluloid Skyline. Random House, New York.

Scott, Otto. (2004, January). Christianity and Capitalism in History. USA Gold. http://www.usagold.com/gildedopinion/Scott.html

Shearer, S. R. (n.d.) Capitalism and Christianity. Antipas Ministries.http://www.endtimesnetwork.com/oldnews/ cap_christ.html

Shearer, S. R. (1998, December). The Elite, Money and the "End of Days":The Economic Network.http://www.antipasministries.com/html/file0000190.htm

Smith, Adam. The Wealth of Nations. 1937 [publisher unknown]. Spong, J. S. (2005, October). A Call for a New Reformation. http://www.dioceseofnewark.org/jsspong/reform.html

Stossel, John (September 1, 2000). Is America Number One? ABC News, New York. [Video S000901-01]

Stratis, G. (2004, October). Dual Morality: Can Christian Ethics Survive in the Workplace? White Paper for Tenure, Nyack College, Nyack, New York.

Swomley, J. (1996, September/October). Cashing in for Christ. *The Humanist, 56*(5), 39.

Symonds, W.C. (2005, May). Earthly Empires: How Evangelical Churches are borrowing from the business playbook. *Time*, 78–88. Tawney, Richard. (1926). Religion and the Rise of Capitalism.
[publisher unknown].

Tewell, T. K. (2003, October). Ministering to the business community. *Theology Today*, 60(3), 344–356.

The Alienist. (2003, August). Christianity in America: Is Capitalism a Biblical Tenet? LitDotOrg. http://www.lit.org/view/ 5985

http://www.ahs.cqu.au/humanities/history/52148/modules/ westC.html

Vinten, G. (2000). Business Theology. *Management Decision, 38*(3), 209–215.

Walle, A.H. (1996). Localized Marketing Strategies and the Bible of International Business. *Management Decision, 34*(7), 5–9.

Weber, Max (1904). The Protestant Ethic and the Spirit of Capitalism.

Welch, E. M. (2003, May). Justice in Executive Compensation. *America, 188*(17), 8–11.

Wosh, P. J. (2002, Autumn). God and Mammon: Protestants, Money, and the Market, 1790–1860. *Business History Review,* 76(3), 583–585.

About the Author

John Laski grew up in the poorer section of Passaic, New Jersey during the mid-50s.

Raised by his maternal grandmother and his Mother, he was determined to not let the lack of a strong male influence affect his upbringing. Developing at an early age a keen sense of observation and critical thinking, John learned to challenge the status quo, be less accepting than others of simple answers and simple solutions, and to strive to push just a bit farther to see what lay beyond the next turn, under the next rock, in the next hidden compartment.

A product of a largely Catholic upbringing and education, it was a natural extension to attend Don Bosco Tech, a Catholic Technical High School in Paterson, New Jersey, and then graduate from Passaic Senior High School. Following almost eight years of active duty during the Viet Nam conflict, with the U.S. Navy, John returned to school graduating from Salve Regina University, Nyack College, with undergraduate degrees, later earning an MBA in Finance from St. Thomas Aquinas College, and a doctorate (DBA) in Finance with a second specialization in International

Management from Nova Southeastern University.

John has worked in international business with Marubeni Corporation of Japan, UVA Machine Company of Bromma, Sweden, then transitioned to Wall Street with Merrill Lynch and Citigroup, and ultimately launched his own firm, leading to his third career in higher education. As an associate professor of finance, international business and management, John has taught at several institutions in adjunct and full time capacities. He had created and implemented an MBA Program in 2002, and is currently working on developing a new MBA program at a state university in New Jersey.

John is married, sharing five children all with varying interests and successes, enjoys golf, photography and target shooting. John spent 10 years involved in local and county government, has been a volunteer fire-fighter for 30 years, and is a freemason, affiliated with a lodge in Newport, RI. John has authored several articles in various academic forums, is currently co-authoring research with Dr. David Hemley, Eastern New Mexico University, and maintains an interest in the integration aspects of "faith and finance." John has been listed over several years in Who's Who in America and Who's Who in Education, and is the recipient over the years of several awards including the Passaic County Medal of Honor for his lifesaving rescue of three fishermen on Greenwood Lake, NY.

www.ingramcontent.com/pod-product-compliance
Lightning Source LLC
Chambersburg PA
CBHW071436180526
45170CB00001B/365